TARGETED
READING
INTERVENTIONS
FOR THE COMMON CORE

CLASSROOM-TESTED LESSONS THAT HELP
STRUGGLING STUDENTS MEET THE RIGORS OF THE STANDARDS

Diana Sisson & Betsy Sisson

📖 SCHOLASTIC

New York • Toronto • London • Auckland • Sydney
Mexico City • New Delhi • Hong Kong • Buenos Aires

DEDICATION

To our parents, Lin and Ruth Sisson, who instilled within us
a love of learning and a lifelong commitment to education

Cover Designer: Jorge J. Namerow
Interior Designer: Sarah Morrow
Development Editor: Joanna Davis-Swing
Editor: Sarah Glasscock
Copy Editor: David Klein

1 2 3 4 5 6 7 8 9 10   40   21 20 19 18 17   16 15 14

CONTENTS

Introduction

Two of the most significant events in the field of education are coalescing in classrooms around the country: Common Core State Standards (CCSS) and Response to Intervention (RtI). The writers who drafted the CCSS emphasize that they designed the standards to address the question of "what" rather than "how." While this approach allows for flexibility in the implementation of the standards, it also leaves many unanswered questions about how to proceed in ways that adhere to the best practices in literacy. Of concern are the estimated one in three students who struggle to learn to read (Greenwood, Kamps, Terry, & Linebarger, 2007). RtI offers the structured, prescriptive format needed to address the standards for these students.

Enacted in 2006, RtI is the culmination of over three decades of federal involvement in special education services. It has two overarching goals: (1) to identify at-risk students and provide intensive intervention prior to the development of severe deficits and disability identification, and (2) to identify students with learning disabilities who are chronically unresponsive to standardized forms of instruction and, instead, necessitate individualized, data-based instruction (Fuchs, Fuchs, & Vaughn, 2008).

One of the primary attributes of the RtI model is the implementation of a multi-tiered approach to student support and intervention (Barnes & Harlacher, 2008; Mellard & Johnson, 2008). Most school systems adhere to three specialized tiers. Tier I centers on core instruction implemented in the classroom. Tier II, for those who don't respond to core instruction, provides targeted interventions in small groups of approximately four to six students, once or twice a week. Students who continue to struggle transition to the intensive interventions of Tier III and work three to five times a week in prescriptive groups of no more than three students.

This text can be used at any of these three tiers, but it is specifically designed for students who struggle at Tier II, or even Tier III. To address the needs of these students, we have carefully and purposefully crafted activities that are

- Research-based
- Aligned to standards
- Proactive and preventive
- Systematic and explicit
- Formatted for small groups of no more than six students

Understanding the importance of academic interventions, we wrote this book to offer insights into what the CCSS standards are, why they are important, and how they can easily be implemented in grades K–3. What do we do with students who cannot master these standards? How do we provide varied instructional supports that are essential for students' success? What approaches will be the most effective for accomplishing these challenges? This book provides the bridge to interventions grounded in clear pedagogical theory and research.

We look at instruction through three distinct lenses. First, we base our work in the developmental psychology theories of Vygotsky, especially focusing on the Zone of Proximal Development (ZPD). ZPD refers to the difference between what a child can achieve independently and what he or she

Targeted Reading Interventions for the Common Core © 2014 by Diana Sisson & Betsy Sisson, Scholastic Teaching Resources

can achieve through guidance and support (Vygotsky, 1962, 1978). We follow this principle by starting instruction at the student's current skill level, providing scaffolded support, and guiding the development of skills that the student will eventually use independently.

Second, we use Bloom's Taxonomy to frame students' cognitive development (Bloom, 1956). Encompassing six levels (knowledge, comprehension, application, analysis, synthesis, and evaluation) of intellectual processing, Bloom's premise is that learners cannot progress to the next level before mastering the previous one. Because of his influence in our approach with struggling readers, we focus on providing systematic activities that build off one another so struggling students can steadily increase their skills through a carefully planned cognitive progression.

Third, the recent work of Heacox in differentiation and her emphasis on the importance of KUDOs has been profoundly important in our focus on structured, scaffolded exposure to concepts and skills (Heacox, 2009). KUDOs is an acronym for what we need students to:

- **K**now (the definitions, facts, and so on, that students memorize for basic recall)
- **U**nderstand (the "big ideas" that students take away from instruction)
- **DO** (the skills and tasks that students are expected to perform independently)

This template allows teachers to scaffold student learning through a systematic approach designed to chunk learning into meaningful parts as students gradually transition to independence. Stemming from Bloom's Taxonomy, KUDOs offers an instructional tool that also helps us critically analyze the essence of the content we want students to master as we reflect on key knowledge that students must acquire, the essential understanding underlying the content, and what specific goals we envision for students.

With more than 30 years of combined experience in the field working with students at every grade level, we believe that, in addition to educational theory, there are certain principles that should guide instructional practice as well. These principles have the power to affect student learning, and more significantly, to ultimately influence performance outcomes. If you look at these principles, or drivers for change, as a sequence of instructional planning, they provide a blueprint for effective interventions.

Principles to Guide Instructional Practice

1. **Focus on the essence of the content.** What exactly are we expecting from our students? At the very core of our instructional goals, what do we want students to be able to do independently? Once you answer those questions, you will have an incisive focus on which to base all of your work.

2. **Link content to personal connections.** Struggling students often feel disengaged from content and fail to see its relevance to their own lives. Add to that their frustration with making meaning from text, and you have a prescription for failure before you begin. To combat that, look for ways to connect the content to students' own experiences. Show them the relevance of the text and its value to them. Make the content important to their daily lives.

3. **Use short pieces of text.** Lengthy pieces of text can be overwhelming to struggling readers. Before you can begin to discuss content and demonstrate a concept, students may have shut down their own learning. How can they understand what you want to teach them if they are

still trying to construct meaning from the words on the page? To remove that barrier, teach from brief texts that appear accessible and manageable to those students.

4. **Chunk the process.** As with the texts themselves, content can appear protracted and difficult to navigate. As you plan how to deliver instruction, think about what you expect learners to do. How can you break that down into pieces where students can focus on only one component? Once you do that, you can show students the sequence of the text in simple steps—rather than as one inexplicable entity.

5. **Engage the senses.** The more ways we engage students' thinking, the greater their ability to practice and retain the content. Can they see it? Can they talk about it with others, both through listening and sharing their own thoughts? Can they complete a performance task in which they create something to demonstrate their understanding? Challenge yourself to design as many formats as possible for repeated exposure. Each instance allows the learning to deepen.

6. **Develop visual representations of content.** Closely linked to engaging the senses, this instructional driver emphasizes illustrations, charts, and graphics that provide explicit explanation of the content. For students who perceive reading as a mysterious, abstract process, visual representations can often furnish the missing link between the expectations we hold for content learning and students' current level of understanding.

7. **Ensure opportunities for success.** What defines a struggling reader? They struggle with text . . . again and again and again. In many cases, this constant sense of failure becomes a self-fulfilling prophecy: *Why bother trying? I am only going to fail.* If this is the mind-set of a student, then nothing you do is going to help until his or her experiences change. How do you do that? You construct opportunities for that student to blossom. Give your students initial activities in which you know they will feel successful, such as those that link the content to their personal lives. It may be through a particularly easy text that you know they can read independently. It may even be through an activity you know they really like. It doesn't matter what you choose. The point is to make certain students succeed.

8. **Incorporate guided practice.** How do basketball players get better? They practice with a coach who observes them in action, shows them how to improve, and steers them in the right direction. How is that different for struggling readers? It isn't. Guided practice is essential if you are going to track what students understand and what they don't, provide ongoing support, and give them the confidence they need to master the content.

9. **Integrate collaborative activities.** An overriding psychological factor that commonly impedes struggling readers is a sense of isolation. They commonly view reading as a solitary task that they must complete alone and unaided. To dispel this mind-set, you should design collaborative activities in which struggling readers work and learn with others.

10. **Supply layered feedback.** Layered feedback, encompassing three levels of instructional support, is absolutely critical for struggling readers. One, when students perform an academic task successfully, you should summarize which skills and thinking they employed in an explicit, clear recap to ensure that they are cognizant of how they achieved success as well as how to replicate that success in other contexts. Two, when students are grappling with a task, you should engage them in a conversation to help them trace their thinking back to the point where their understanding broke down. Determining where the disconnect between their knowledge and the content happened allows students to see that they did have partial success. Also, if you do

not find the disconnect, you cannot help students improve because you do not know where their understanding fractured. Three, if students fail at a particular task, you need to talk them through the process. Show them how to achieve success in small, manageable steps.

How to Use This Book

We have interwoven these instructional drivers throughout the book, providing a detailed explanation of each of the College and Career Readiness Anchor Standards for Reading with interventions in both literature and informational text.

Each chapter of this book highlights one anchor standard. We also recommend the KUDOs necessary for promoting powerful instruction for that standard. Then we analyze the standard's pedagogical purpose and rationale for inclusion in high-quality instruction and follow that with the transitional steps for mastery that illustrate how students progress throughout the grades with an increasingly more complex and sophisticated skill set.

Although this text centers on the work of K–3 students, we have included transitional steps to grade twelve to demonstrate the continuum of learning each student must acquire throughout his or her academic career and, equally, to emphasize how important the work you do is—not just to the learning of students today, but also as a foundation for the learning these young students must accomplish tomorrow.

Each activity in a chapter includes the underlying principles for how these interventions provide prescriptive support for the needs of struggling students, along with a list of any materials you'll need to carry out these engaging, hands-on interventions. The activities align to the Common Core State Standards; each chapter begins with kindergarten expectations and then progresses to first, second, and finally, to third grade. Instructionally, you can implement the activities that correspond to the grade-level expectations of your students, or you can move back to previous activities if you feel they lack foundational skills from prior grades. As you begin to implement these interventions in your classroom, use the focus questions at the bottom of each activity to scaffold students' thinking and understanding of the content. You can decide how many focus questions to ask; they are designed to help you structure your students' interactions with the text and/or activity. Note that we often provide variations of the same question to help expand students' experience with these kinds of questions.

For each activity that requires a text, we offer general suggestions for selecting a suitable text, but we rarely recommend a specific title. We have made this decision thoughtfully and intentionally for the following reasons.

First, we don't want our readers to infer that a suggested text is the "best" possible resource. You shouldn't feel compelled to purchase or locate a text in the belief that the activity cannot be done without that specific text. In actuality, you can utilize texts you already have access to. You should be able to implement these activities immediately without having to locate additional resources.

Second, we have designed these activities to be flexible, fluid, and applicable to a range of genres, topics, reading levels, and grades. Suggesting a specific title would negate this aim and limit the text's appropriateness for students you target for intervention. A title we suggest may be too difficult for students in your group. Similarly, a title we recommend may not be challenging enough for your students. Furthermore, if your students lack foundational skills, it is good instructional practice to discover where the gap exists in their understanding and scaffold from that entry point—rather than simply beginning at their current grade-level placement.

Third, our hope is that this book will empower you to think about how you can use your resources in varied ways to provide effective, prescriptive instruction. What's more, we believe that students should be cognizant that books—be they fiction or nonfiction—can be viewed through multiple lenses. Rather than searching for a new text for every standard, consider that a single text can speak to numerous standards. For example, we often use the fairy tale, "Cinderella," for initial discussions about text as it is a universal narrative told in over 300 cultures and it allows student to focus on the literacy skills we are building and not on comprehending a new story. As we show below, you can use this one story as an exemplar text to teach nearly all the Common Core State Standards.

Standard 1 (Reading for Details): *At what time must Cinderella return from the ball? Why do you believe that Cinderella suddenly reveals herself to the prince when he is in her home with her missing shoe? Use details from the text to support your answer.*

Standard 2 (Theme/Summarization): *What is the moral of this story? Use details from the text to support your answer. What happens in this story? Be sure to include all of the important events.*

Standard 3 (Narrative Elements): *Why do you think Cinderella's stepmother treats Cinderella the way she does? Use details from the text to explain your answer.*

Standard 4 (Vocabulary): *The word "ball" has multiple meanings. How is it used in this text? Use details to explain your answer.*

Standard 5 (Text Structure): *What is the text structure of this story? How do you know? How would the story change if it were a different text structure? Would it change your understanding of the story?*

Standard 6 (Point of View/Author's Purpose): *From what point of view is the story related? How would the story change if it were related through the point of view of Cinderella's stepsisters? For what purpose do you think that this story was originally told? Be sure to use details from the story to explain your thinking.*

Standard 7 (Diverse Text Formats and Media): Read the story. Then watch a video of it. *How are the story and the video alike? How are they different? Use specific examples to explain your answers.*

Standard 8 (Evaluate Arguments in a Text): Not applicable to literature

Standard 9 (Comparing and Contrasting Multiple Texts): Read two different versions of "Cinderella." *Does the theme of the story change between the two versions of the story? Use details from both texts to explain your answer.*

Standard 10 (Variety of Genres and Levels of Text Complexity): Use "Cinderella" as a scaffold to guide students in reading a more complex text.

That's how easy it is to use one text for multiple standards. Not only will concentrating on one text make your instructional planning easier, but it will also demonstrate to students how to read a text more deeply and with more consideration. So, please, utilize these activities to offer prescriptive interventions that best meet the needs of your students.

In the Appendix, you'll find an introduction to the Common Core State Reading Standards (CCR1–10) and KUDOs as well as a list of additional resources. All of these materials support the goals of this text as well as the work that you do.

* * *

The landscape of the American classroom is changing. We cannot simply react; we must actively engage in reform and seek out ways to redesign our instructional practice—especially with our most vulnerable students. We hope this book will help you along your way.

CHAPTER 1

Reading for Details Using Both Literal and Inferential Understanding

Read closely to determine what the text says explicitly and to make logical inferences from it; cite specific textual evidence when writing or speaking to support conclusions drawn from the text (CCSS, p. 10).

What students need to . . .

KNOW

- Logical inferences
- Textual evidence
- Conclusions

UNDERSTAND

- Conclusions are drawn by combining a reader's prior knowledge with information from the text.
- Conclusions must be drawn from relevant details from the text.
- Having support for a conclusion is an important aspect of drawing a conclusion.

DO

- Read text closely.
- Make logical inferences.
- Cite specific textual evidence.
- Support conclusions drawn from text.

Pedagogical Foundations

As a building block in developing reading comprehension skills, CCR1 falls within the first cluster of standards, Key Ideas and Details. Before students can determine craft and structure, integrate knowledge and ideas from text, or read and comprehend complex literary and informational text, they must first understand the explicit message of selected texts and be able to draw conclusions about what they read. As such, it is imperative that teachers focus on literal comprehension to ensure that students take the first step to independent reading (Basaraba, Yovanoff, Alonzo, & Tindal, 2013; Herber, 1970; Kintsch & Rawson, 2005; Nation, 2005; Perfetti, Marron, & Foltz, 1996; Van Kleeck, 2008). Following an explicit understanding of key details and the author's message, students must learn to think deductively and link their conclusions to evidentiary support.

• • • • • • • • • • •

Transitional Steps for Student Mastery

Beginning in kindergarten, students should be able to answer questions about key details in a text and transition to specific inquiries regarding who, what, when, where, why, and how by the end of second grade. While students in grade three provide explicit support for their responses, grade four marks the first year that inferential thinking appears as a benchmark for reading achievement. This focus intensifies in grade seven when students must cite multiple pieces of textual evidence to support their thinking, and then in grade eight when students must analyze which of the selected evidence most strongly supports their analysis of both the explicit text message and their inferential reasoning. By grade eleven, students must add to their accumulated skills the ability to determine where selected texts leave matters uncertain.

Prompting Cards

Asking detailed questions to young students can be a challenge. They often see the "big picture" without attending to specifics. For a struggling reader, answering these detailed questions can exacerbate an already trying situation. We believe that students need to make connections to the content so the "big picture" has relevance to content learning. Learning cannot take place unless we can link what students know to that unknown that they are to master. We look for ways to apply the content to students' own lives before we expect them to apply that understanding to content. In the activity below, we follow that principle with the additional support of scaffolded learning.

Materials and Preparation

- Prompting Flashcards (p. 12)
- Colored cardstock or paper
- Scissors

Copy and cut out a set of the following Prompting Flashcards: Who? What? When? Where? (Note: You will use the complete set of these cards in other activities.)

Directions

Ask students to describe one thing that they did over the weekend. As they tell their stories, use the flashcards for prompting. Hold up the "Who?" card. Ask one student who was with him or her. Then, hold up the "What?" card. Encourage that student to tell what happened. Next, hold up the "When?" card. Ask, "When did this happen?" Finally, show the "Where?" card, and ask "Where were you?" Continue using the Prompting Flashcards as you ask other students to share their stories.

Focus Questions

1. Who is in the story?
2. What happens in the story?
3. When does the story happen?
4. Where does the story happen?

PROMPTING FLASHCARDS

Who?

What?

When?

Where?

Why?

How?

Detail Scramble

Before asking students to identify details in a text, give them the details. This is another step in the scaffolding process. Looking at details, talking about them, and manipulating them encourages struggling readers to become comfortable and confident. Then . . . have students try their new skills with a real text

Materials and Preparation

- Detail Cards (p. 14)
- Colored cardstock or paper
- Scissors

Copy a set of the Detail Cards and cut them out.

Directions

Talk with students about how *who, what, where,* and *when* tell readers important parts of stories. Explain that today they will practice seeing how these little parts make up big stories.

Mix up the Detail Cards and give them to your students. Have them identify all the **WHO** cards. Then ask them to identify the **WHAT** cards. Ask students to match a **WHO** card with a **WHAT** card and make up silly stories about the character(s) and event. Next, tell students to identify the **WHERE** cards, and use them to extend their stories. Do the same for the **WHEN** cards. Finally, challenge students to see if they can organize all the categories of cards into realistic stories.

Focus Questions

1. Who is in the story?
2. What happens in the story?
3. When does the story happen?
4. Where does the story happen?

DETAIL CARDS

WHO	WHAT	WHERE	WHEN
Jaheem	built sandcastles	at the beach	in the morning
Lisa and John	played	in the park	after school
The family	went to the zoo	in New York	on Saturday
I	read a book	in my room	this afternoon
Jose	took a walk	in the park	last weekend
Mrs. Johnson	had dinner	in the kitchen	at 6:00

 Targeted Reading Interventions for the Common Core © 2014 by Diana Sisson & Betsy Sisson, Scholastic Teaching Resources

Details Pop Up

For primary students, we like to incorporate as much kinesthetic activity and sensory detail as possible. Utilizing multiple modalities in ways that are engaging and fun provides the perfect means for young students to learn. This activity allows them to "pop up" from their seats as they hear key details. Simple—but fun!

Materials and Preparation

- A narrative text
- Prompting Flashcards (p. 12)
- Colored cardstock or paper
- Scissors

Copy and cut out a complete set of Prompting Flashcards.

PROMPTING FLASHCARDS	
Who?	What?
When?	Where?
Why?	How?

Directions

Read a book aloud to your students. Give each student one of the Prompting Flashcards. Assign the following task: "As you listen to the story, 'pop up' out of your seat when you hear your card being discussed in the text. For example, if your card says 'Where?' pop up when you hear the setting of the story described. If your card says 'What?' listen for what happened."

Focus Questions

1. Who is in the story?
2. What happens in the story?
3. At what time does the story take place?
4. Where does the story happen?
5. Why does . . . ?
6. How does . . . ?

Coding Details

When students first attempt to use newly acquired skills with real text, we provide three key scaffolds: (1) modeling, (2) guided practice, and (3) chunked activities. Chunking is an essential bridge in developing skills. Perhaps the most common characteristic that struggling readers share is the sense of being overwhelmed when encountering text. The best away to alleviate that anxiety is to chunk what these students are reading into smaller, less intimidating pieces. They can still get to the finish line . . . just one step at a time.

Materials and Preparation

- A narrative text
- Sticky notes

Prepare a set of sticky notes with the words who, what, when, where, *and* how *for each student. Select a book for a shared-reading activity with your students.*

Directions

Tell students that you are going to read a story to them. After reading the story aloud, ask students to identify who was in the story. When students locate the answer in the text, instruct them to attach their *who* sticky note beside that location. (Students may place their sticky notes at different places in the text.) Stop to support students' understanding. Reinforce their answers and draw their attention back to the story to ensure that each student has located the correct passage. Follow the same process for the rest of the categories: *what, when, where*, and *how*.

Focus Questions

1. Who is in the story?
2. What happens in the story?
3. When does the story happen?
4. Where does the story happen?
5. How does . . . ? (e.g., How does the character solve his or her problem?)

Story Cards

So many classroom assignments can feel threatening to struggling students. Faced with daunting tasks, these students often do not know where to begin and quickly give up. This activity chunks the task into small, manageable pieces and allows students to focus on one single element of the text. Students work in small groups, so they also benefit from working collaboratively and build off others' understanding to strengthen their own comprehension.

Materials and Preparation

- Prompting Flashcards (p. 12)
- Colored cardstock or paper
- Scissors

Copy and cut out enough Who?, What?, When?, Where?, Why?, and How? cards so each student in the group will have one card.

Directions

Place the cards facedown on the table. Tell students to select one card. Explain that the word on the card will be their only focus while they read the story, or you read it aloud to them. At the end of the reading, ask the focus questions. Have students respond based on their story card and identify specific evidence from the text that supports their answers. If any Prompting Flashcards are left over, distribute them to individuals (or pairs) in the group and continue the activity.

Focus Questions

1. Who is in the story?
2. Where does the story take place?
3. When does the story take place?
4. What is the story about?
5. How . . . ?
6. Why . . . ?

Marking Details

Engagement is an essential principle in working with struggling readers. When students are unable to understand the words on a page and answer questions, they often step back and withdraw. When that happens, you cannot remediate effectively because students do not believe they can do what you ask. So, the first step is not to teach a skill. Begin by engaging students. We want them physically engaged, not just intellectually engaged. This activity uses crayons and colors to do just that!

Materials

- A copy of a story for each student
- A blue, red, green, and orange crayon for each student

Directions

After reading aloud the text, tell students that you want them to really think about the story and to mark it up to show what they understand. To do that, they are going to underline who was in the story in blue, what happened in red, where the story happened in green, and when it happened in orange. Go through each detail one at a time, and make certain that students are finding the correct details from the story to answer your focus questions.

Focus Questions

1. Who is in the story?
2. What happens in the story?
3. Where does the story happen?
4. When does the story happen?

Text Tie-Ins

Struggling students often do not make links between posed questions and the textual evidence that should lead them to a logical, accurate answer. One way to help them see that connection is through a symbolic physical representation.

Materials

- A narrative text
- Sentence strips
- A 1-hole punch
- Short pieces of yarn

Directions

After reading a text to your students, ask them the focus questions. For each answer, they must write the evidence from the text on one sentence strip and their answer on another strip. Explain how answers must link to what the text actually says—the "evidence" from the text that they find. As you discuss the text, show students how to hole-punch the sentence strips and tie the evidence strips and answer strips together with yarn.

Focus Questions

1. Who is in the story?
2. Where does the story take place?
3. When does the story take place?
4. What is the story about?
5. How . . . ?
6. Why . . . ?

Text Cutouts

We firmly believe that students need repeated exposure to as many different contexts as possible to cement their understanding of content. This activity provides just such an opportunity as students physically manipulate pieces of text when they consider what information each piece tells the reader.

Materials

- A copy of a passage that has clearly identifiable elements of who, what, where, when, why, and how for each student
- Scissors

Directions

Ask students to read the passage, cutting out the pieces of text that relate to each of the relevant elements. Be sure to provide time for students to share their text cutouts with their classmates.

Focus Questions

1. Who is the passage about?
2. Where does the passage take place?
3. When does the passage take place?
4. What is the passage about?
5. How . . . ?
6. Why . . . ?

● Build a Story

Working collaboratively can greatly aid struggling students because it enables them to explore content with others while providing a "safety net" that they lack when working alone. This activity fosters partnerships and encourages students to share their understanding in a safe environment.

Materials and Preparation

- Prompting Flashcards (p. 12)
- Colored cardstock or paper
- Scissors

Copy and cut out enough Who?, What?, When?, Where?, Why?, and How? cards so each student in the group will have one card.

Directions

Place students in groups of six. Each person in the group takes on one type of detail (i.e., who, what, where, when, why, or how) and is responsible for "building" that part of a group story. Start with the Who? card. This student must decide who the characters in the story will be. He or she names them, describes them, and sets them up for the action of the narrative. Then move on to the What? card. This student decides what the problem will be. The student with the Where? card highlights the setting (e.g., inside/outside, day/night, season, and so on). The student with the When? card describes the time frame of the story (present/past/future, time of day, and so on). The student with the Why? card decides why the character is experiencing the problem suggested by the student with the What? card. Finally, the student with the How? card determines how the problem is resolved.

Focus Questions

1. Who is the story about?
2. What is the problem in the story?
3. Where does the story take place?
4. When does the story take place?
5. Why is the character experiencing this problem?
6. How is the problem solved?

Every Little Detail Counts!

Student-generated writing is an essential step in learning. If students can transfer their skills from one context to another (i.e., from reading to writing), then they have truly gained proficiency. Self-created texts also help students become more aware of their own learning and to express their understanding in a way that we can assess.

Materials

- Paper and pencils

Directions

Ask students to write an original story, making sure to include all the narrative elements: characters, setting, plot, and resolution. Afterward, instruct students to exchange their stories with a classmate to see if they can find the answers to the focus questions below.

Focus Questions

1. Who is the story about?
2. Where does the story take place?
3. When does the story take place?
4. What is the story about?
5. How . . . ?
6. Why . . . ?

CHAPTER 2

Theme/Main Idea and Summarization

> *Determine central ideas or themes of a text and analyze their development; summarize the key supporting details and ideas* (CCSS, p. 10).

What students need to . . .

KNOW

- Main idea
- Central ideas or themes of a text
- Key supporting details and ideas
- Events
- Summarization

UNDERSTAND

- Main ideas are the overarching messages that authors want readers to walk away with from the text.
- Theme is a universal truth presented by the text.
- Theme is a central idea that unifies the text.
- Literary elements (e.g., characters, setting, plot) contribute to the development of the theme.
- Theme typically is inferred—not directly stated by the author.
- Texts may contain more than one theme.
- Both main ideas and themes are developed from supporting details and ideas.
- Retelling is the precursor to summarizing. To retell, the reader recalls large portions of the text, listing important details in chronological order. To summarize, the reader highlights only the most essential details.

DO

- Identify the main ideas and supporting details in a text.
- Determine the central ideas or themes of a text.
- Analyze the development of central idea or themes.
- Retell stories using key supporting details.

Pedagogical Foundations

CCR2 focuses on students' abilities to identify themes in fiction and central ideas in nonfiction as well as to construct concise summaries of content in both genres—which all require determining importance in text. Determining importance has become an expected skill of effective readers (Alvermann, Swafford, & Montero, 2004; Gill, 2008; Johnson, 2005; Keene & Zimmermann, 1997; McGregor, 2007; Miller, 2002) as it is "central to making sense of reading and moving towards insight" (Harvey & Goudvis, 2000, p. 118), and nowhere else is it more needed than in Anchor Standard 2. This standard requires the ability to differentiate between pertinent information and extraneous details and utilizing this distinction to develop broad generalizations about a text in order to identify its theme. Theme is significant. Because narrative texts provide lessons about life that are universal and common to all cultures, students must understand that all narratives have a theme. If a reader does not grasp the theme of a narrative, then he or she will have lost the power of the story—reducing it to a simple narrative for entertainment purposes.

Of equal importance is the ability to express an understanding of theme in clear written language. For students in the early grades, this means identifying the theme of a text and producing a retelling (in grades one through three) or a summarization (grades four and up). These written aspects demand that the reader both identify the theme and provide evidentiary support through a summarization of the key events of the narrative. In the case of informational text, students must grasp the central idea of a text in order to be cognizant of the author's intent for the reader. They must also recognize that central ideas can only emerge from tying together key details in a coherent union of thought. Thus, with both fiction and nonfiction, students need to find the inherent connections in the text and appreciate how these connections work in tandem with the author's words and ideas.

Finally, students link their skills in identifying theme and central idea with their ability to summarize as a means of producing a broad understanding of the text.

●●●●●●●●●●●

Transitional Steps for Student Mastery

With literary text, kindergarten students need only retell a text; however, grade-one students must add to that retelling with a demonstrated understanding of the central message or lesson. Beginning at grade three, students use those skills with specific literary genres. For example, students in grade three look specifically at fables and folktales; in grade four, mythology is added, while grade five includes drama and poetry. A transition occurs in grade four when students begin to summarize the text. The level of sophistication increases again in grade six when students analyze the theme or central message throughout a text and then provide a summary free of personal opinions or judgments. By grade eight, students should be able to identify the theme or central idea's relationship with the characters, setting, and plot. Students in grades nine and ten consider how specific details in a text shape the theme or central idea. At the end of high school, students in grades eleven and twelve should be able to reflect on how two or more themes or central ideas interact and build upon one another to form a complex text.

With informational texts, students in kindergarten through grade two identify the main topic and key details with texts of increasing complexity. Students in grades three through five transition from main topic to main idea. Grade four marks the first time students summarize text; in prior grades, they retell only. Determining how main ideas are conveyed and analyzing their development becomes the focus for students in grades six through eight. Students in grades nine and ten reflect on how key ideas may shape or refine the text. By the end of grade twelve, students consider multiple central ideas and how they interact with one another.

● Main Idea Bags

Identifying the main idea can be very abstract and demand a more globalized grasp of a text than other comprehension tasks do. For young children, the first step is to develop the actual meaning of the concept of main idea and supporting details. As a scaffolding step, we find it helpful to provide students with the "details" of the text through real objects related to it. This ensures that students focus on how details work together to build the main idea—without the added pressure of addressing text.

Materials and Preparation

- An informational book
- A Main Idea Bag for the book: paper bag and objects

Find concrete objects that pertain to the book you've selected and place them in the paper bag. Here are some examples of the contents of Main Idea Bags for books about the beach and about school.

Beach Bag	School Bag
Shells	Children's book
Sand	Pencil
Beach ball	Paper
Sand pail and shovel	Eraser
Beach hat	Backpack

Directions

Display the Main Idea Bag. Explain to students that each item in the bag is connected to the book that you are about to read to them. Bring out each item, discuss what it is, and challenge students to guess what the book may be about, based only on the items from the bag. As students make predictions about the book, use the appropriate language to teach them about this concept of main ideas and details. For example, you might say, "These items are all details, or small things, about this book. The items, or details, show us the main idea. Main idea is what the book is mainly about. Use the details to find the main idea!"

Finally, read the text and ask students how the items in the Main Idea Bag helped them prepare for the book. Did knowing the main idea help them understand the book better? Are there other items that they would select to help someone understand the main idea of the book?

Focus Questions

1. What is a detail from the bag?
2. Can you find that detail from the bag in the book?
3. What is the main idea? How do you know?
4. Do the items help you better understand the book? How?
5. Do the items help you decide on the main idea of the book? How?

Main Idea Clues

Students commonly struggle to determine the main idea, but they often become overwhelmed by the amount of information in the text and confused about what information is important and what isn't. A simple strategy to help students determine main idea is to teach them where the "clues" are in a text. This activity focuses on specific aspects of a text that provide strong support for determining the main idea before students even begin reading. It is a pre-reading strategy that effectively encourages students to be thinking about the main idea of the text before engaging with it.

Materials

- A narrative or an informational book

Directions

Discuss with your students that certain parts of a book give "clues" to its main idea. It is their job as readers to look for those clues and use them to identify the main idea. First, draw students' attention to the title of the book. Ask them to predict what the main idea of the book may be based on its title. Second, focus on the front cover illustrations. Again, ask students to use the illustrations to confirm or change their predictions. Third, guide them through a brief picture walk of the book and then have them make a final decision. Finally, read the book with students and ask them to confirm their predictions based on the clues.

Focus Questions

1. What is the title of the book? What do you think the main idea of the text may be?

2. What do you see on the front cover of the book? Is the front cover clue similar to the title clue? What do you think the main idea of the text may be?

3. What do you see in the illustrations in the book? Do these provide clues like the title and front cover do? What do you now think the main idea of the text may be?

4. Are your clues right? How do you know?

Raise Your Hand for Main Idea!

Students often select a main idea without having the textual details to support their selection. Thus, a critical aspect in developing students' understanding of main idea is to ensure that they understand that main ideas cannot exist without supporting details. Main ideas and supporting details are symbiotic and must function together if they are to support the readers' understanding of the text.

Materials

- An informational text with a strong main idea and clearly written supporting details
- A sheet of drawing paper for each student
- Crayons

Directions

Explain that main ideas and supporting details are much like a hand. Each finger works together to help the hand work. In reading, each supporting detail helps the main idea work.

Ask students to draw the outline of one of their hands on the sheet of drawing paper. Read the informational text. As you read, guide students to write down a supporting detail on each traced finger. After the reading, ask them to determine what the main idea may be based on their "fingers." Instruct students to write the main idea on the palm of their traced hand.

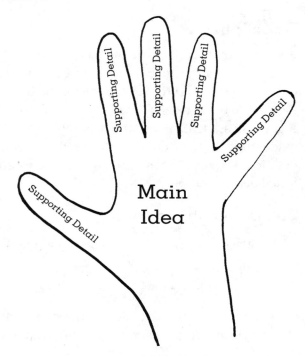

Focus Questions

1. What is a supporting detail from the text?
2. Looking at the supporting details, what do you think the main idea is? Why?
3. Does each supporting detail support the main idea? How?

● Life Lessons

It is often difficult for students to see the real-world applications of what they learn in school. Understanding that students are more successful with content when they can see its connection to their own lives and the world around them, we typically use activities that allow us to talk with students about concepts before we introduce any text. This serves several purposes. First, it bridges the connection from school to world. Second, it takes the anxiety of reading out of the learning process until students have at least a rudimentary grasp of the underlying content. Third, it acts as a scaffolding technique through which students build their skills in a safe zone before we ask them to apply their newfound knowledge in an instructional context.

Directions

Lead a group discussion on the rules that students follow at home (e.g., do their homework, clean their room), in school (e.g., don't run in the hallways, raise their hand before calling out), and in life (e.g., look both ways before crossing the street). Then ask students why we have these rules. What lessons do we learn from these rules? Make the point that we have rules based on the lessons learned when people did not follow those rules. Lessons occur naturally throughout our lives. They also occur in the work of authors. Authors tell stories that share the lessons of life. End the discussion with a review of some of the students' favorite books and what lessons they have learned from these stories.

Focus Questions

1. Why do we have this rule? Why do you think it became a rule?

2. This story teaches . . .

3. What lesson does this story teach?

● Secret Message

Identifying the lesson of a story often proves to be a huge stumbling block for struggling readers. While they are attempting to make meaning at the most literal level, we are asking them simultaneously to determine what message the author is trying to impart through the telling of the narrative. While we may not use the word "theme" until the intermediate grades, these early years furnish an essential foundation in that developmental process as demonstrated by the Common Core's use of the terms "lesson," "moral," and "central message" prior to the more advanced concept of theme. As for a specific strategy, begin by emphasizing the problems and solutions in stories through guided practice with familiar texts. It is the solution that shows readers the lesson or moral of the story. The author crafts the narrative so we learn from characters' experiences, and we grasp these lessons by how characters' problems are resolved.

Materials

- A story with an explicit theme, such as a fable or fairy tale

Directions

This strategy works best if you provide some frontloading prior to implementing it. First, begin by reaffirming the four central components of a story: characters, setting, problem, and solution. Then model these components through familiar stories. After discussing several stories, revisit them and draw students' attention specifically to problems and solutions. Explain that authors have secret messages in their stories that help readers learn lessons, such as messages related to the importance of family, overcoming difficulties, being rewarded for hard work, and so on. It is our job as readers to find those messages.

Demonstrate how we can discover the secret messages from the ways in which characters' problems are resolved. Select a story that you have read with students, or read a new story that contains an explicit theme, such as a fable or a fairy tale. For example, in the story of Cinderella, the main character experiences many hardships (e.g., an uncaring stepmother and cruel stepsisters who treat Cinderella as a servant in her own home) and faces the problem of not being allowed to attend the ball. Cinderella's problem is resolved by her fairy godmother, who provides clothes and transportation to the ball, where Cinderella meets the prince and falls in love. The secret message, or theme, of this narrative is that good things happen to good people, because Cinderella remains a kind person throughout the story and is ultimately rewarded for her goodness.

End by asking students what lesson they learned from the solution to the problem in a particular story.

Focus Questions

1. What lesson does this story teach?

2. This story teaches that . . .

3. What is the moral of this story?

4. What is the central message of this story?

Extension Activities

* If students require a stronger personal connection, begin by recounting a brief story from your own life. Highlight the problem and the solution from the story, and then share the lesson you learned from this experience. Then ask students to share a story from their own lives. Be sure to emphasize that this story must have a clear problem and solution. Ask students in the group what lesson(s) they learned from listening to the story. Does it match the lesson that the student telling the story learned?

* If students respond well to real-world applications, ask them to recount a story from television or cinema. What is the problem? What is the solution? What lesson can we learn from the solution? This extension activity can offer significant insight into building awareness of theme as it highlights that authors in all media, (e.g., books and television and cinematic presentations) hope to teach life lessons.

Fabled Lessons

When teaching story lessons, we always incorporate fables—specifically *Aesop's Fables*. They constitute the perfect genre to illustrate this concept. Why? The fables contain brief text, few characters, simplistic action, and an easily observable moral.

Materials and Preparation

- A book of fables
- Index cards and a marker

Select several fables as read-alouds. Choose three or four fables for each team and write the moral of each fable on a card.

Directions

Scaffold the use of the fables by beginning with read-alouds. As a group, discuss what lesson the character learns from the problem (what the moral of the story is). Gradually withdraw your guidance and ask students if they can determine the theme of a fable by themselves. As a last step, move students into teams, and give each team a small collection of fables (perhaps three or four) and cards detailing the moral of each one. Direct them to match the fable with the moral.

Focus Questions

1. Who is the main character?
2. What is the problem?
3. What is the solution to the problem?
4. How does the character react to the problem and its solution?
5. What lesson does the character learn?
6. What is the moral of the story?

 Targeted Reading Interventions for the Common Core © 2014 by Diana Sisson & Betsy Sisson, Scholastic Teaching Resources

Picture Cards

Before we begin remediation, we always focus on two specific aspects of instruction: (1) the appropriate text for the task and (2) developing a strategy that provides a high expectation for student success. In the case of retelling, we choose a highly predictable text with strong story grammar. There should be no surprises for students. We also develop retelling prompts that are highly engaging, student-friendly, and supportive of the retelling process. Story cards can be a great way to begin for the young reader.

Materials and Preparation

- A predictable book with a clear narrative sequence
- Cardstock, markers, scissors

Create a series of picture cards that highlight each major event in the book's plot.

Directions

Read aloud the book. Distribute the picture cards to students. Instruct them to organize the pictures in the correct sequence and retell the story with the help of the cards. (The use of picture cards as a scaffolding tool will allow struggling readers to gain practice with the skill of retelling as well as offering a visual support to facilitate recall.) As students gain proficiency, slowly take away this scaffolding. Retain the initial event and the concluding event, and ask students to retell the middle portions of the story. Then take away the concluding event and, finally, the initial event.

Focus Questions

1. What happens first, second, third . . .?
2. What happens in the story?
3. What happens first?
4. What happens in the middle of the story?
5. What happens at the end of the story?

Tag! You're It!

Students often struggle with what to include when retelling a story. Being able to identify the basic framework of a story greatly enhances students' understanding of narratives and improves their ease in retelling. This activity borrows from the game of Tag: Each student shares his or her part of the story and then "tags" the next student. Start by focusing on the beginning, middle, and end of a story.

Materials and Preparation

- A story with a clear sequence (e.g., a fairy tale)
- Index cards
- Marker

Create a set of "beginning," "middle," and "end" cards for each group.

Directions

Move students into groups of three. Give each student in a group a different card. Explain that their only task is to listen for what their card says as you read the story. For example, a student with the "beginning" card will focus on what happens at the beginning of the story, and so on. After sharing the beginning of the story, this student turns to the student holding the "middle" card and says, "Tag, you're it!" That student describes the middle of the story, then turns to the student holding the "end" card and says, "Tag, you're it!" (This creates a game atmosphere and also provides students with a concrete understanding of how each part of the beginning, middle, and end works together.)

At the completion of the activity, line up each group according to the three story components. Challenge each group to retell the story with each student retelling his or her piece of the story.

Focus Questions

1. What happens at the beginning of the story?
2. What happens in the middle of the story?
3. What happens at the end of the story?

Retelling Frames

Retelling a story can be highly frustrating for students who are using the majority of their cognitive resources to make meaning at the word level. After students expend all their energy in decoding words and comprehending individual sentences, asking them to retell an entire narrative can simply be too much. For these students, we look for ways to provide a framework through which we can support their understanding of a story by having key events already in place—as place markers for their own memories.

Materials and Preparation

- A story with a clear sequence
- A retelling frame for each student

Create a retelling frame for your students to use with the story. See the examples below.

Directions

Instruct students to think about the most important events in the story as you read it. If necessary, focus their attention on the beginning and end of the story. For students who struggle to differentiate key events, you may also stop at various points in your reading to highlight events and point out their placement in the text—beginning, middle, or end.

After finishing the read-aloud, provide your students with a retelling frame. You can tailor the frame to meet whatever needs your students have. Here are some examples:

* Show the initial event and the concluding event and ask students to supply the middle action.

* List the initial event and ask them to add the succeeding action.

* List all the major events, encouraging students to add the lesser events.

After students complete the retelling frame, ask them to retell the story using the frame as their guide.

Focus Questions

1. What is the beginning event in the story?
2. What happens first in the story?
3. What happens in the middle of the story?
4. After that, what happens?
5. What is the ending event?
6. How does the story end?

Sequence Chain

Reading is a very cerebral process, so we always try to incorporate as many hands-on, kinesthetic activities as possible. The Sequence Chain is one of our favorite strategies to help young readers physically retell stories. It is fun, engaging, and provides a built-in support system to assist students in retelling narrative texts. First, creating the sequence chain requires that students reflect on the story, write the main events on individual strips of construction paper, and then attach them together—symbolizing the interlinking nature of single events to create a complete narrative. Second, students can look at and touch their individual "chain links" as they orally retell the story. If students falter in their retelling, they have the visual representation of the main events as a scaffolding system.

Materials

- A story with a clear sequence
- Different colors of construction paper cut into strips
- Pencils, markers, or crayons
- Tape

Directions

Set the purpose for the lesson by explaining to your students that their task is to listen for the major events as you read a story aloud. After the read-aloud, work with them to determine events at the beginning, middle, and end of the text. Guide your students' understanding by asking them to write each major event on a strip of construction paper. Work slowly through the events as students record their event "links" for the story. After students complete links for each of the major events, help them create their sequence chain by linking and taping the strips. Then ask students to retell the story, using their chain for support if they stumble.

Focus Questions

1. Tell me what happens in the story.

2. What happens first in the story?

3. Then what happens?

4. After that, what happens?

5. What does the character do then?

6. How does the story end?

Extension Activities

⋆ If students require a stronger personal connection to the text, encourage them to draw a picture on the individual links they've recorded.

⋆ If students can complete a basic retelling, move their thinking forward by helping them analyze how each link affects the telling of the story. You can do this by taking away individual links or moving the links around and questioning how these changes affect the telling of the story.

CHAPTER 3

Narrative Elements and Sequence of Events

Analyze how and why individuals, events, and ideas develop and interact over the course of a text (CCSS, p. 10).

What students need to . . .

KNOW

- Individuals
- Characters
- Events
- Ideas

UNDERSTAND

- Authors may convey information about characters through direct characterization (literally telling the reader what the character is like) or indirect characterization (providing clues through how a character looks, speaks, acts, thinks, and feels).
- Characters' actions propel the plot forward.
- Individual events function in a cause-effect chain that weaves the plot of a story into a unified whole.
- Individuals, events, and ideas are connected in text.
- Ideas evolve within a text as the author prepares them to support his or her purpose in writing.

DO

- Analyze how characters, events, and ideas develop and interact.
- Analyze why characters, events, and ideas develop and interact.
- Describe the connection and relationship among individuals, events, and ideas.

Pedagogical Foundations

Narrative elements play a crucial role in understanding and analyzing narrative text (Bukowiecki & McMackin,1999; Duke & Pearson, 2002; National Reading Panel, 2000; Reese, Suggate, Long, & Schaughency, 2010; Snow, 2002; Stetter & Hughes, 2010; Taylor, Abler, & Walker, 2002). These elements (characters, setting, and events) remain the same despite text complexity. Their level of sophistication, however, does change alongside the text and its expectations for the reader. Thus, students in kindergarten can identify the main characters, setting, and events of a story. What may become more problematic is their ability to understand how these elements interact with one another and ultimately influence the story. This connection among key elements holds true in informational text as well, as students strive to see the relationship among individuals, events, and ideas.

●●●●●●●●●●●

Transitional Steps for Student Mastery

Students in kindergarten through grade two focus on characters, settings, and events. Beginning in grade two, this focus shifts to a heavier emphasis on characters and how they respond to events and challenges. Building on this foundational understanding of narrative structure, grade-three students consider how character actions influence the sequence of the story. By grades four and five, students provide in-depth descriptions of characters/settings/events, and then are able to compare or contrast these literary elements using specific details from the text (grade five). Grades six through eight highlight a specific narrative element with a greater degree of sophistication and skill. For example, the grade-six curriculum looks at plot; grade seven considers the interaction of literary elements; and grade eight analyzes the effect of specific events and dialogue on story development. That concentration continues in grades nine and ten with a deeper reflection on complex characters and, in grades eleven and twelve, with a thorough analysis of how an author's choices affect story elements.

In contrast, informational text expectations revolve around individuals, events, and ideas. It begins in kindergarten and first grade where students describe the connection among these three components of nonfiction writing. Grade two adds the skills of sequential steps. By grade four, students begin to explain the relationships among these elements. Students in grades six through twelve analyze individuals, events, and ideas with closer scrutiny and more sophisticated evaluation.

All About Me

Narrative elements are the building blocks necessary to constructing a story. As a means to draw parallels between students' lives and the stories they read, asking children to tell stories from their own lives makes a very concrete connection.

Materials

- Chart paper and marker

Directions

Before beginning to analyze texts to identify narrative elements, ask your students to tell a story from their own lives. Pick a topic and encourage them to share (e.g., favorite birthday memory, meeting their best friend, their first day of school, and so on). Have two or three students share their reflections, and then focus on the patterns that are emerging. Each story has characters, settings, and events. As more storytellers begin to share, chart the narrative elements contained in their stories and then guide students as they begin to distinguish among these elements for themselves.

Focus Questions

1. Who are the characters in this story?

2. What is the setting of this story? Where does it happen? When does it happen?

3. What are the main events of the story? What happens first? Next? Then? Finally? How does the story end?

No Words Needed!

In identifying narrative elements, students can easily become mired in a book's text and illustrations. With so much to process, they may lose focus of the individual elements of the story. A simple remedy for this is to use wordless picture books, which have no text to discern nor adult voice to listen to—just the pictures themselves. There is one focus and one modality, eliminating all other distractions.

Materials

- A wordless picture book

Directions

Invite students to identify the characters in the picture book based solely on the illustrations. Next, ask them to describe the setting. Encourage them to be mindful of the details in the illustrations. As you move through the book, ask questions about what is happening in the pictures. Be sure to guide students' construction of the story around key events to ensure a coherent narrative.

Focus Questions

1. Who are the characters in this story? What do they look like? What do you see in the picture?

2. What is the setting in this story? What do you see?

3. What is happening in the pictures?

4. What happens at the beginning of the story?

5. What happens in the middle of the story?

6. What happens at the end of the story?

● 3 . . . 2 . . . 1 . . . The Stage Is Yours!

Socio-dramatic play is critical for developing cognitive, socio-emotional, and physical skills in young children. It encourages students to explore the world and provides a critical link between their lives and stories when studying narrative elements. Before drawing or writing about stories, acting out aspects of narratives is a powerful transitional step in students' learning. We have found these types of strategies to be highly popular with primary students and immensely beneficial in their literary development.

Materials

- A narrative text for students to act out

Directions

As you work with students to identify characters, settings, and events, give them opportunities to act out specific narrative elements. To make it more exciting and motivating, have others guess which element is being acted out. For example, whisper to each child what he or she will be portraying. One student may pretend to be a particular character from the story. Another may simulate what the setting looks like, while other students act out major events from the text. As each student "takes the stage," the others in the group try to guess who or what is being represented.

Focus Questions

1. Who are the characters in this story?

2. What is the setting in this story?

3. What are the main events of the story?

Story Bags

Story bags provide a strategy that is collaborative, hands-on, and engaging. They are simple to create, but they encourage students to think more deeply about stories and to share their understanding with others.

Materials and Preparation

- A different narrative text for each group
- A small paper bag for each group
- A variety of objects that relate to the text
- Construction paper, index cards, and markers and crayons

Write the title and the name of the author on the outside of each bag. You may also opt to have students write this information on the bags.

Directions

Select a story to read with your students. Designate each member of the group to be responsible for a different narrative element of the story.

- ＊ Characters
- ＊ Setting
- ＊ Events/Plot
- ＊ Problem
- ＊ Solution

After handing out the Story Bags, ask groups to decorate them. Then explain that each member of the group will find an object that relates to his or her narrative element and place it into the bag. For example, a student who is responsible for setting may bring a shell if the story occurs at a beach. If a student cannot locate an appropriate object, he or she may draw a picture of the narrative element on construction paper or describe the element on an index card.

The student whose task it is to relate the plot completes a set of numbered events cards that explains the events in the story. Make sure to remind students that the solution of the story must resolve the problem; therefore, those objects should directly relate to the problem. After the story bag is complete, have each group retell its story based on the objects in the bag. Individual groups can do this on their own, or groups can share their story retellings with one another.

Focus Questions

1. Who are the characters in this story?

2. What is the setting in this story? Where does it happen? When does it happen?

3. What happens at the beginning of the story? In the middle? At the end?

 Targeted Reading Interventions for the Common Core © 2014 by Diana Sisson & Betsy Sisson, Scholastic Teaching Resources

● Storyboard

Storyboards offer an excellent visual representation of the narrative elements found in stories. They also allow students to chunk information into smaller bits, encouraging them to focus on only one element at a time.

Materials

- A narrative text
- Storyboard Template (p. 42) for each student
- Pencils, crayons, or markers

Directions

In order to incorporate multiple modalities (visual, auditory, and kinesthetic), have students read or listen to a story. They then discuss who the main character is, what the setting is, and what the main events of the story are. After students have completed the discussion with necessary prompting to ensure their understanding, ask them to create a storyboard.

To create the storyboard, students fold the Storyboard Template vertically into three equal sections. In the first section, they illustrate the character; in the second section, they draw the setting; and, in the last section, they draw three pictures depicting the three major events of the story—beginning, middle, and end. As students gain proficiency, the scaffolding of a pre-discussion is withdrawn and they create the storyboard independently.

Focus Questions

1. Who is the main character?
2. Describe the characters in the story.
3. What is one word that best describes this character?
4. What is the setting of the story?
5. What are the main events of the story? The beginning? The middle? The end?
6. How does the main character respond to . . . ?
7. What does the main character do when . . .?

Extension Activity

✶ Variations include using the storyboard as a means to facilitate retelling and utilizing it to allow students to tell a story that others in the group have not read or heard before.

Name _____ Date _____

STORYBOARD TEMPLATE

CHARACTER	SETTING	EVENTS
		Beginning
		Middle
		End

● SHOW Me the Details!

Details can be the most vital aspect of a narrative. Unfortunately, they can also be the easiest to lose in the shuffle of text, illustrations, and discussions. In the primary grades, we devote our attention to chunking instruction as well as to selecting the materials we use. In this activity, students listen for story details in the absence of written text and illustrations. At the same time, however, we challenge our younger students to listen carefully so that the illustrations they create based upon their listening will rival those in the book. Even at a young age, students love a challenge!

Materials

- A picture book
- Blank sheets of paper and pencils, markers, or crayons for drawing

Directions

Read a story aloud to your students without letting them see the illustrations. Instruct them to draw what the main character looks like based on what they hear. Reread the text, asking students to draw an additional picture of what they think the setting might look like. On your third rereading, stop directly after the first main event, giving students time to complete a detailed drawing of that event. Continue until you reach the next main event (or the middle action), and provide time for students to draw it. End by stopping at the last main event (the end of the story) and having they draw this as well.

Do a group share of students' finished illustrations. Have each student display his or her illustrations and describe the details. Then show what the book's illustrations look like. With students' pictures displayed and the book open, lead a discussion about which details the students' illustrations included from the text, as well as which details they incorporated into their own pictures.

Focus Questions

1. How would you describe this character?

2. How would you describe the setting?

3. How would you describe what is happening at the beginning of the story?

4. How would you describe what is happening in the middle of the story?

5. How would you describe what is happening at the end of the story?

If I Were in Your Shoes

Asking young students to describe how characters react to events and challenges in a story can be problematic. Not only is this an analytical skill that students may not have developed, but it also requires a certain degree of empathy to grasp why people respond to situations in the way that they do. In order to equip students to identify such reactions, we find it helpful to have them first think about what they would do in the situation. This kind of reflection reinforces rational thinking and a reasonable assessment of characters and their responses.

Materials

- A story about a character who faces a challenge

Directions

Read the story with your students. Point out a particular event or challenge from the text and talk about how you would have responded. Next, talk about the way the character reacts. Is it the same as your response? Different? Why? Then continue to another event or challenge in the story. Ask students how they would have responded. Probe for a rationale for their reactions. What would motivate them to react in such a way? Is it realistic? Would it make sense in the telling of this story? Finally, ask students to identify how the character actually responds. What comparisons can they make between the character and themselves that would produce such responses? Use the diagram below to provide a concrete image for this task.

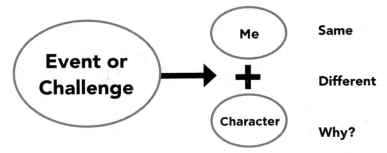

Focus Questions

1. What would you do if this happened to you? Why? How does the character act? Why do you think you would have acted in the same way? Why do you think you would have acted differently?

2. How would you respond to a challenge like this? Why?

3. How does the character respond to this challenge? Why do you think he or she reacts this way?

4. Which response do you think is better? Would you ever act like the character in the story does? Why?

Character Traits Word Bank

When asking a reader to describe a character, you invariably hear words like "nice," "good," "happy," and so on. Lacking a strong vocabulary, many students cannot adequately portray a character. The first thing we do is provide students with a word bank of potential character traits. This encourages them to integrate their vocabulary knowledge with story content. Combining these two elements actually increases students' understanding of story, character development, and real-world connections.

Materials

- Character Traits Word Bank (p. 46) for each student
- A story that features a strong character

Directions

First, teach students the list of words in the Character Traits Word Bank. You may want to chunk these words to ensure that your students master them. One of the best methods for students to acquire vocabulary is for you to focus on how the word relates to their lives and experiences, its links to familiar stories, its associations to film and television characters, and its use in real-world situations. Exposure to the word in multiple contexts strengthens students' understanding and retention. Next, introduce the story. Ask students to identify one word from their bank to describe the character. Be sure also to require them to provide textual evidence that supports their word choice.

Focus Questions

1. How would you describe this character? Use evidence from the text to support your answer.

2. What word best describes the character? List details from the story to support your choice.

3. How do the character's traits affect the sequence of events in this story? Include evidence from the text to support your answer.

Extension Activity

✱ If students exhibit extreme difficulty in identifying character traits, offer them a choice of three or four traits from which to choose.

CHARACTER TRAITS WORD BANK

afraid	enthusiastic	lonely
angry	excited	loyal
bossy	fair	mean
brave	faithful	mischievous
calm	fearless	miserable
careless	foolish	polite
caring	friendly	proud
cautious	frustrated	quiet
childish	greedy	respectful
clever	grouchy	responsible
committed	guilty	rude
confident	happy	sad
confused	hard-working	scared
creative	helpful	shy
cruel	honest	spoiled
curious	humorous	stingy
daring	impatient	strong
dependable	independent	stubborn
determined	intelligent	thoughtful
dishonest	jealous	upset
easygoing	kind	weak
embarrassed	lazy	wicked

Targeted Reading Interventions for the Common Core © 2014 by Diana Sisson & Betsy Sisson, Scholastic Teaching Resources

The Power of Motivation

As educators, we often ask students why characters do what they do. On the surface, this seems like a relatively simple question. It isn't. The ability to discern the "why" in a story typically stems from two sophisticated reading skills: (1) drawing conclusions about the text and (2) analyzing character motivation. When we provide instruction and support for inferential thinking without focusing on what motivates characters to behave as they do, this creates a gap in student understanding and, more important, in their ability to evaluate text.

Materials

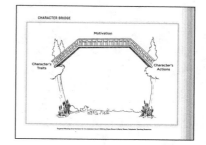

- A narrative text
- Character Bridge (p. 48) for display

Directions

Motivation is a complicated concept, making it difficult to teach. Use the Character Bridge reproducible to explain to students that a character's traits create the motivation for him or her to act. In effect, motivation can be understood through one's traits or characteristics (e.g., greedy, friendly, brave). In turn, readers can use these to predict the character's actions in the story. Working in reverse, a character's actions can be explained by his or her motivation, which answers that deceptively complex question of "Why?"

Focus Questions

1. How would you describe this character? Use evidence from the text to support your answer.

2. What word best describes the character? List details from the story to support your choice.

3. How do the character's traits affect the sequence of events in this story? Include evidence from the text to support your answer.

4. Why does the character . . . ? What motivates him or her to . . . ?

CHARACTER BRIDGE

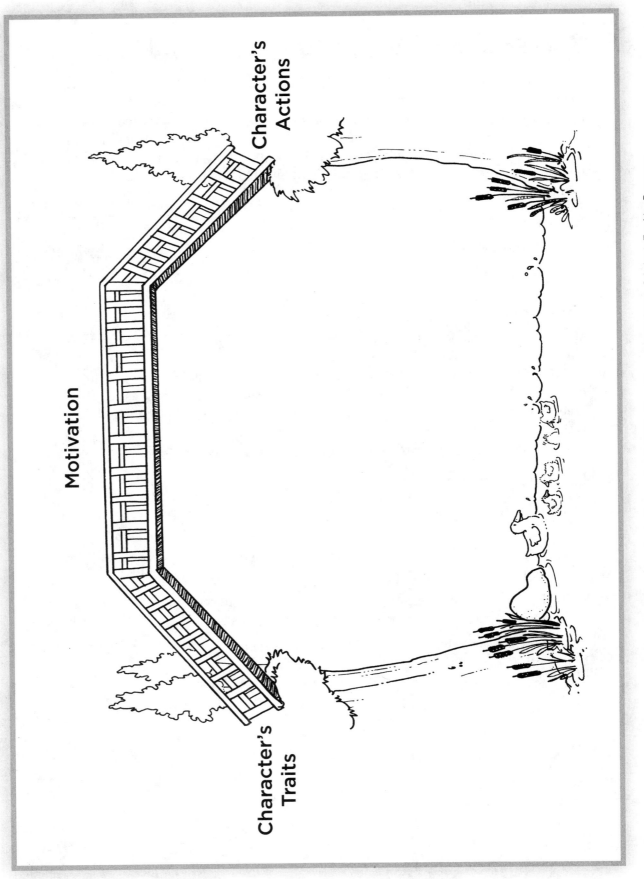

Character's Actions

Motivation

Character's Traits

Targeted Reading Interventions for the Common Core © 2014 by Diana Sisson & Betsy Sisson, Scholastic Teaching Resources

Action . . . Reaction

Narratives follow a cause-and-effect structure. One action leads to another action, which leads to another action, and so on. Unfortunately, struggling readers often see these actions as isolated without noting their effect on the sequence of events. We find that one of the most powerful techniques for reinforcing the cause-and-effect concept is through a guided retelling of a familiar story.

Materials

- A story that students know well

Directions

Provide a guided retelling of the story for your students. As students recount the story, encourage them to think what the actions of the characters are and what happens in the story because of these actions. Emphasize that each action has an effect that causes another action. Move the entire narrative along using the word *because* to demonstrate explicitly the cause-and-effect nature of characters' actions on the sequence of events in stories. The example at the right shows a retelling of "The Tortoise and the Hare."

Focus Questions

1. What happens first in the story? What does the character do?

2. What happens next because of what the character does?

3. Because of that, what happens?

4. What happens at the end of the story because of the character's actions?

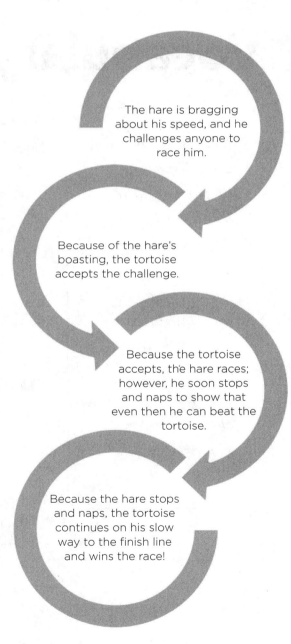

The hare is bragging about his speed, and he challenges anyone to race him.

Because of the hare's boasting, the tortoise accepts the challenge.

Because the tortoise accepts, the hare races; however, he soon stops and naps to show that even then he can beat the tortoise.

Because the hare stops and naps, the tortoise continues on his slow way to the finish line and wins the race!

CHAPTER 4

Vocabulary in Context

Interpret words and phrases as they are used in a text, including determining technical, connotative, and figurative meanings, and analyze how specific word choices shape meaning or tone (CCSS, p. 10).

What students need to . . .

KNOW

- Words and phrases as they are used in a text
- Technical meanings (specialized vocabulary in a given field)/Connotative meanings (words associated with a term)/Figurative meanings (words used to describe something by comparing it to something else, e.g., simile, metaphor, personification, idiom, onomatopoeia, hyperbole)
- Word choices
- Meaning/Tone

UNDERSTAND

- Multiple meanings of words and phrases are contextually bound to the text.
- The specific words that an author chooses can affect both the meaning and tone of the text.

DO

- Interpret words and phrases as they are used in a text.
- Determine technical, connotative, and figurative meanings.
- Analyze how specific word choices shape meaning or tone.

Pedagogical Foundations

CCR4 explores the significance of word sense in developing reading comprehension skills. One of the best-understood relationships in literacy is the understanding that vocabulary is inherently linked to reading comprehension (Baumann, 2005; Beck & McKeown, 2007; Juel & Deffes, 2004; Kieffer & Lesaux, 2007; Lubliner & Smetana, 2005; Richek, 2005; Scarborough, 2001; Stahl & Nagy, 2006; White & Kim, 2009). In fact, students' knowledge of words is the greatest predictor of their reading comprehension (Baumann, Kame'enui, & Ash, 2003).Without the ability to identify words and their meanings in context, readers will struggle to read with deep understanding (Armbruster, Lehr, Osborne, & Adler, 2010; Artley, 1943; Carlisle, 2007; Fukkink & de Glopper, 1998; Goodman, 1965; Graves & Watts-Taffe, 2002; Nagy & Anderson, 1987; Smith, 1974; Sternberg, 1987). This precept relies on students gaining skills in contextual analysis and integrating that awareness with other meaning-making skills in their repertoire.

●●●●●●●●●●●

Transitional Steps for Student Mastery

Developing word sense begins in kindergarten with students answering questions about unknown words. By first grade, students focus on words that suggest feelings or appeal to the senses, and second graders consider how words furnish the rhythm and meaning to texts as well as topic or subject-area words found in informational text. Distinguishing between literal and nonliteral language becomes the focus in third grade, while fourth grade emphasizes how to identify meaning through context. This focus continues in grades five through twelve with additional work on figurative language (beginning in grade five) and then connotative language (beginning in grade six). Grade eight also includes analogies and allusions. At a more sophisticated level, figurative and connotative meanings continue to be a focus area in high school with added emphasis on the cumulative impact of specific word choices on meaning and tone (grades nine and ten) and multiple meanings (grades eleven and twelve).

Graphic Cues

In reading instruction in the primary grades, we focus a great deal of our energies on teaching students to use cueing systems. We begin with the graphic cues (picture clues) to help them understand unknown words. Explicit instruction and modeling with this system demonstrate for struggling readers what strategies able readers employ to make meaning from text.

Materials

- A picture book
- Letter identification cards (optional)
- Magnetic letters (optional)
- Alphabet books and songs (optional)

Directions

Begin by reminding your students about everything that you can learn from a book by just looking at the pictures. To reinforce this understanding, look at the cover of the text you've chosen. Ask the focus questions below.

Focus Questions

Pre-Reading

- What do you see on the front cover of this book?
- What do you think will happen in the story? Why?
- The title of the book is _____. Look at the front cover again. What do you think the story will be about now? Why?
- Look at the pictures inside the book. What is happening? How do you know?
- Who is in the story? Where is it happening? When is it happening?
- What is happening in the book? What do you see?

During Reading

- What is happening? What do you see the character doing?
- What do you think will happen now? Why?
- See if there is a clue in the picture that helps you with the word.
- Does it look right? Is that the word you expect to see?
- You have the first sound in the word. Do the pictures give you any clues to help you read the word?

- This word says _____. Do you see anything in the pictures that shows that word?

- The story says _____. Where do you see that happening in the pictures?

Post-Reading

- Look at the front cover again. What does the picture show? Were you right about your prediction? Why?

- Look back at the pictures. Can you tell me the story now?

Extension Activity

* Students can also benefit from a grapho-phonemic cueing system in which they focus on print matter, e.g., the words themselves. Activities within this cueing system emphasize letter-sound relationships and connections between what is seen and heard, such as with explicit instruction on phonological principles; for example, help students build grapho-phonemic skills through the use of letter identification cards, magnetic letters, and alphabet books and songs.

Syntactic Cues

The syntactic cueing system arms struggling students with a powerful strategy to make meaning, and perhaps more important, to repair meaning when comprehension breaks down. For students to utilize this cueing system, however, they must grasp correct language structures and grammatical patterns in English. This is often challenging for struggling readers—but it's incredibly difficult for second-language learners. We suggest that you integrate read-alouds and repeated readings throughout your instructional day to encourage these students to listen to and recognize these natural language patterns.

Materials and Preparation

- A familiar book
- Sentence strips
- Marker
- Scissors
- Paper clips or envelopes

Choose several sentences from the book. Write each on a separate sentence strip, cut it into individual phrases, and mix up the pieces. Paper clip the phrases for each sentence together or place them in a separate envelope. For the second phase of the activity, write a sentence on a sentence strip and then cut apart the words.

Directions

One strategy to encourage the use of syntactic cues is to break apart authentic text, chunking sentences, phrases, and words into meaningful parts. To begin, read a familiar story with your students. Then show them the sentence strip phrases and explain that the phrases form a sentence from the story. Ask them to put the phrases together into one complete sentence. Guide students in their thinking as they work to reassemble the sentence.

After students have had several successful experiences at the phrase level, have them continue the same process by reconstructing sentences from the individual words. Pause periodically and ask students to share their thinking process, making sure to model yours as well. Emphasize the method you use to decide how the words fit together.

Focus Questions

1. Which group of words goes first? Next? How do you know?
2. Read the sentence for me. Does it sound right? How do you know?
3. If I move the words around, will the sentence still make sense?

4. What clues tell me this is the beginning of a sentence? What do we do for the first word of a sentence?

5. What clue do I have that this is the end of a sentence? What do we do at the end of every sentence?

Extension Activity

* The semantic cueing system relies heavily on contextual analysis. In this system, students use contextual words and sentences to determine the meaning of an unknown word. They employ four specific types of context clues:

(1) The definition context clue explicitly defines the meaning of the word in the text. (e.g., Geography, *which is the study of places,* is a fun subject.)

(2) The synonym context clue suggests the meaning by using a simpler term. (e.g., Pachyderms, *or elephants,* are large animals.)

(3) The antonym context clue indicates the meaning through the use of an opposite or unlike term. (e.g., I thought my teacher would assign me a huge amount of homework, *but* the homework was just *miniscule.*)

(4) The gist (or inference) context clue explains meaning through implied relationships. (e.g., The weather forecaster said it would be *raining cats and dogs.* He was right. It was raining really heavily.)

Incorporating this cueing system provides an avenue for students to discover the meaning of unknown words—in whatever text they are reading. Therefore, PRACTICE, PRACTICE, PRACTICE! If you do not reinforce context through daily instruction, students will not use it independently.

Pragmatic Cues

The pragmatic cueing system emphasizes the function and purpose of language. Its power derives from giving students' insight into how text works. Although this system incorporates a number of different aspects of textual understanding, we tend to focus on story grammar, author studies, and genre explorations. In this context, we want to provide our students with prior knowledge of a particular type of story that will equip them to have expectations for future texts. This background knowledge allows struggling students to connect the known (previously read stories of a similar nature, e.g., common story grammar or genre) to the unknown (a story they are currently reading with a similar story grammar or genre). In turn, they begin to build a framework from which they can make meaning.

Materials
- Fairy tales and stories in other genres

Directions

Provide your students with regular exposure to a variety of genres. We suggest that you begin with fairy tales, a genre that has a clearly defined grammar and predictable story elements. As you read these stories with your students, point out their common features. Continue this emphasis as students read similar texts, drawing their attention to what they can expect to read.

Focus Questions

1. How does the story begin? How is this like the other stories that we have read?

2. This story begins with "Once upon a time . . . " Have we seen other stories begin this way? Which ones? Can you give me some examples?

3. Where does this story take place? Is that similar to any of the other stories we have read?

4. How would you describe this character? Is she (or he) like other characters? How?

5. The story ends with ". . . and they lived happily ever after." Have we read any other books that ended this way? Which ones?

6. Think about other stories similar to this one. What do you think those stories might say?

 Targeted Reading Interventions for the Common Core © 2014 by Diana Sisson & Betsy Sisson, Scholastic Teaching Resources

Feelings Collage

Using photographs of real people to identify the feelings of story characters give students a firmer grasp of the feelings being described in a text. This activity asks students to search specifically for feelings, fostering authentic discussion about emotions, developing the vocabulary associated with feelings, and creating points of reference for later literacy work.

Materials

- Magazines
- Scissors
- Glue
- Poster backing
- Sentence strip
- Marker or pen
- A story or poem that features examples of feelings

Directions

Instruct students to cut out photographs from the magazines that show feelings (e.g., a person smiling shows happiness) and glue them onto the poster backing to create a feelings collage. As they do this, write each feeling on a small piece of a sentence strip and affix it to the appropriate photograph. After students finish their collage, read the story or poem you selected and encourage students to identify any words or phrases that match the feelings displayed in their collage.

Focus Questions

1. What feelings do you see in this picture?
2. What word or phrase do you hear that shows us the character's feelings?
3. What word or phrase do you hear that shows us the author's (or poet's) feelings?

Sensory Words

As we work with primary students to develop their language acquisition, beginning with sensory words provides the perfect springboard for vocabulary development. These words have relevance to young children's lives, and you can easily explain them through stories and facial expressions. Of further importance, sensory words are common throughout early childhood literature, so young readers who master them improve their reading and become more sophisticated in their understanding of text.

Materials

- Sensory Words (p. 59)
- Picture books and/or poems with a strong usage of sensory words
- Materials for experiential activities (optional: see below)

Directions

Review with students the five senses, and then brainstorm words that suggest or appeal to the senses. (See the following page for examples.) Next, read the text you selected and model for students which words are sensory in nature. Then read other appropriate texts and ask students to identify when they hear a reference to a particular sense by using nonlinguistic cues. For example, they may point to their eyes when a word appeals to vision, to their ears when a word appeals to hearing, to their noses when a word appeals to smell, to their tongues when a word appeals to taste, and hold out their hands when the word appeals to touch. This will allow students to be more kinesthetic and you to check immediately for student understanding. If students exhibit a severe lack of background knowledge with sensory vocabulary, frontload these words with experiential activities— showing them visual terms, mimicking the sounds of auditory terms, bringing in items that have particular smells, having a taste test, and providing objects that demonstrate terms associated with touch.

Focus Questions

1. What words do we know that show what we see?

2. What words do we know that show what we hear?

3. What words do we know that show what we smell?

4. What words do we know that show what we taste?

5. What words do we know that show what we touch?

6. Does _____ show what we see, hear, smell, taste, or touch? How do you know?

Name _____ Date _____

SENSORY WORDS

See	Hear	Smell	Taste	Touch
white	crash	sweet	salty	wet
black	laugh	burnt	sour	icy
red	stomp	fishy	hot	sharp
blue	yell	perfumed	buttery	sticky
green	whisper	moldy	sugary	soft
orange	sing	spoiled	bitter	furry
brown	buzz	scented	fruity	dry
pink	chuckle	musty	bland	cool
yellow	thunder	piney	ripe	wet
silver	clap	dry	tasteless	silky
round	snap	fresh	medicinal	sandy
square	rustle	briny	crisp	fuzzy
oval	sigh	earthy	fruity	gritty
crescent	cheer	fresh	savory	velvety
triangular	whistle	damp	tangy	damp
rectangular	bark	sharp	sugary	hairy
large	bray	rancid	vinegary	waxy
immense	bleat	dank	oily	warm
small	hiss	acrid	rich	wooly
tiny	crow	sickly	creamy	thick
short	whine	pungent	rotten	tepid
tall	bang	gamy	stale	steamy
wide	giggle	putrid	yummy	fragile
narrow	chatter	spicy	zesty	hard

Active Alliterative Activities

Kids love tongue twisters. Recognizing this as a great hook, we usually start here in our study of alliteration and its effect in poetry. As soon as our students understand what alliteration means and can create alliteration on their own, we then examine how alliterative phrases influence both the rhythm and the meaning of poems.

Directions

Start with a simple tongue twister, such as this popular one from Mother Goose.

> *Peter Piper picked a peck of pickled peppers;*
> *A peck of pickled peppers Peter Piper picked;*
> *If Peter Piper picked a peck of pickled peppers,*
> *Where's the peck of pickled peppers Peter Piper picked?*

Read several additional examples with your students to ensure that they grasp the nature of alliteration. Try other tongue twisters, such as the one below.

> *How much wood would a woodchuck chuck*
> *If a woodchuck could chuck wood?*
> *As much wood as a woodchuck could chuck,*
> *If a woodchuck could chuck wood.*

Then encourage students to create a tongue twister around their own name, like the example below.

> *Sue was a serious student who studied on the sly.*

After you have provided several experiences with alliteration, draw your students' attention back to the alliterative phrases and reflect on how the alliterative words influence the poems' rhythm and meaning: *For example, if I change the words "on the sly" to "on the weekend," would the alliteration about Sue sound any different? Is it as enjoyable? Does the rhythm stay the same? Is it different? Why? Does the change in words affect the meaning of the line in any way? How?*

Focus Questions

1. Which words have the same beginning sounds?

2. What would happen to the rhythm of the poem if I took out this word and added a word that did not have the same beginning sound? Does it sound better? Is it as interesting to hear?

3. What would happen to the meaning of the poem if I took out this word and changed it to another word? Does the meaning of the line change in any way?

Rhyming Partners

Although recognizing rhymes proves to be effortless for most students, some struggle valiantly to hear these paired sounds—often to no avail. We find that the ability to make such auditory distinctions is enhanced by collaboration with other students along with kinesthetic activities that engage thinking and offer repeated exposure.

Materials and Preparation

- Index cards
- Marker

Create a set of cards with pairs of rhyming words.

Directions

Give each student one rhyming word card. Next, direct all students to go around the room saying their word to classmates, searching for the classmate whose word rhymes with their own. When they find their partner, both students should hold up their cards. After students have found their partner, they read their words and explain which letters in the words make them rhyme.

Focus Questions

1. Do these words rhyme? How do you know?
2. Which letters make the words rhyme?

You Can Say That Again

Noticing is the precursor to understanding. That said, before students can grasp the implications of repeated lines to understand an author's meaning, they must first recognize the repetition. Students can then use these repeated lines or phrases as placeholders to revisit the text and reflect on the significance of the placement of the words as well as the power they add to the overall meaning of the passage.

Materials

- A story, poem, or song that contains repeated words or phrases
- Wikki Stix®

Directions

Give students the text and Wikki Stix. Instruct them to read it, using the Wikki Stix to underline repetitions. Then lead a discussion about why the author, poet, or songwriters may have placed those words there and repeated them.

Focus Questions

1. Can you find any words or phrases repeated in this story, poem, or song?

2. Why do you think the author, poet, or songwriter repeats the words?

3. Why do you think the author, poet, or songwriter places the repeated words in that particular place in the text?

4. How does the repetition affect the meaning?

5. Would the meaning change if the repeated words were taken away? Why?

6. Would the meaning change if the repeated words were moved to a different place in the text? Why?

 Targeted Reading Interventions for the Common Core © 2014 by Diana Sisson & Betsy Sisson, Scholastic Teaching Resources

Idiomatic Match-Up

Authors employ idiomatic expressions to create more imaginative writing and vivid imagery, but struggling readers often come to a grinding halt when they encounter such expressions. The best way to get these students to appreciate and understand such phrasing is to expose them to as many examples as possible so that they begin to see how idioms can make reading more interesting and how context can help readers determine their meaning. We suggest that you look for examples in authentic literature, highlighting the meanings and modeling their use in other contexts. Explicit instruction is also essential for your struggling students to acquire an understanding of idiomatic expressions.

Materials and Preparation

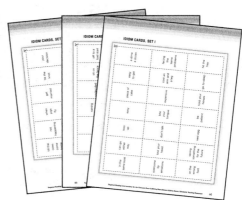

- Idiom Cards (pp. 65–67) for each group
- Scissors
- Sheets of paper and drawing tools

Copy and cut out the three sets of Idiom Cards.

Directions

Give explicit instruction in each of the idiomatic expressions through a set protocol:

- ✱ Provide a clear, literal meaning for the idiomatic expression.
- ✱ Use the expression in real-life examples.
- ✱ Encourage students to make a personal connection to the expression.
- ✱ Ask them to sketch out a drawing that illustrates the meaning of the expression.

Focus Questions

1. What does this card mean?
2. Which card has a matching meaning?
3. Can you explain the meaning of this card in any other way?

Extension Activities

- ✱ **Idiom Match:** Familiarize your students with this game:

  Step 1: Shuffle all the Idiom Cards.

  Step 2: Place cards facedown in neat rows.

Step 3: Students take turns turning over two cards. If the cards match (i.e., the idiom with its literal meaning), they leave the two cards face up. They also win one point and receive an additional turn. If the two cards do not match, students turn over the cards so they are facedown. They receive no points, and the next student takes a turn.

Step 4: When all the cards are facing up, the game is finished. The student with the most points wins the game!

* **Draw an Idiom:** This activity is based on Old Maid, the classic children's card game, which is categorized as a "scapegoat game" because the goal is to avoid drawing a particular card.

Step 1: Shuffle all the Idiom Cards well.

Step 2: Deal the cards to each student in the group. If some students receive additional cards due to the number of cards in the deck and the number in the group, that will not affect the play.

Step 3: Students look for pairs in their hand of cards (i.e., the idiom with its literal meaning). They place the pairs face up on the table.

Step 4: The first player then places his or her hand facedown on the table. The student to the left selects one card from the hand. If that card makes a match with one of his or her cards, that student places the pair face up on the table.

Step 5: This student then places his or her hand facedown on the table, and play continues in a clockwise direction.

Step 6: Play continues until each idiom has been matched to its meaning.

Step 7: If there are only two players, the winner is the student who is not holding the **IDIOM** card.

Step 8: If there are more than two players, the winner is the student who is not holding the **IDIOM** card and who has accumulated the most pairs of matching cards.

IDIOM CARDS, SET 1

a dime a dozen	facing the same problems	hit the hay
easy to get	cost an arm and a leg	go to sleep
piece of cake	expensive	hold your horses
easy	bite your tongue	be patient
toss up	don't talk	nest egg
can go either way	lose your head	saving something for the future
in the same boat	overcome by emotions	on the wrong foot

IDIOM CARDS, SET 2

off to a bad start	nervous	start at the beginning
sit on the fence	saved by the bell	hear it through the grapevine
undecided	saved at the last possible second	hear a rumor
raining cats and dogs	under the weather	on the same page
storm	sick	in agreement
on pins and needles	start from scratch	ball in your court

IDIOM CARDS, SET 3

your decision	a long time	miss an opportunity to do something
tie the knot	in a blue moon	tip of the iceberg
get married	rarely	just the beginning
when pigs fly	see eye to eye	hold your horses
not happening	agree	wait
till the cows come home	miss the boat	**IDIOM**

Idiom Pictionary

As concrete thinkers, younger students often find idioms incomprehensible and perceive only the literal meaning of these phrases. Capitalizing on the wordplay that students of this age enjoy, idiom pictionaries are ideal for exposing young readers to idioms, fostering a love for the silliness that comes from reading them literally, and creating a personal storehouse of idiomatic meanings.

Materials

- Blank sheets of paper
- Pencils, markers, and crayons

Directions

For the Idiom Pictionary, select common idioms that you want your students to understand. Each page of the Idiom Dictionary will follow the same format:

* Write the idiom at the top of the page.
* Draw a line down the middle of the page. On the right-hand side, draw what the idiom literally says. On the left-hand side, draw what the idiom actually means.
* At the bottom of the page, use the idiom correctly in a sentence.

Focus Questions

1. What does the idiom sound like it means?
2. What does the idiom actually mean?

 Targeted Reading Interventions for the Common Core © 2014 by Diana Sisson & Betsy Sisson, Scholastic Teaching Resources

CHAPTER 5

Text Structure

Analyze the structure of texts, including how specific sentences, paragraphs, and larger portions of the text (e.g., a section, chapter, scene, or stanza) relate to each other and the whole (CCSS, p. 10).

What students need to . . .

KNOW

- Structure of texts
- Specific sentences, paragraphs, and larger portions of text
- Section/chapter/scene/stanza

UNDERSTAND

- Text structure affects the way a reader should approach a text.
- Text structure is deliberately and purposefully designed by the author to present content in the best possible way.
- Parts of the text (e.g., sections, chapters, scenes, and stanzas) must work collaboratively to create a seamless whole message; each part of the whole has a purpose.

DO

- Analyze structures found in texts.
- Analyze text parts, including sentences, paragraphs, chapters, scenes, and stanzas.
- Determine how these parts fit together and function symbiotically as a whole.

Pedagogical Foundations

CCR5 focuses on text structures and their import for assisting readers in their general understanding and deep comprehension of texts. It is imperative that students grasp that every text they encounter is based on a particular structure or organizational pattern. Recognizing a text's organization ultimately aids students in how they approach that text and understand its purpose in providing information (Bakken & Whedon, 2002; Duke & Pearson, 2002; Dymock, 2007; Hall, Sabey, & McClellan, 2005; Mahdavi & Tensfeldt, 2013; Meyer & Ray, 2011; Williams, 2005; Williams, Hall, & Lauer, 2004). In effect, identifying the structure of a piece of text is tantamount to frontloading students' reading experience. It helps them determine what is important. What's more, when meaning breaks down, readers can stop and think how the text is organized and see whether there is something in the organizational pattern that will help them better understand what they are reading.

●●●●●●●●●●

Transitional Steps for Student Mastery

The recognition of narrative text structures begins in kindergarten with a simple understanding of different types of texts (e.g., storybooks and poems) and continues into first grade where students differentiate between fiction and nonfiction texts. It is not until second grade that students must be able to identify the overall structure, focusing on the beginning, middle, and end. By third grade, students work on parts of stories (chapters), dramas (scenes), and poems (stanzas). This learning strengthens in grade four with an emphasis on the major differences among poems, drama, and prose, and grade five highlights how chapters, scenes, and stanzas fit together, as well as form the overall structures of these texts. By grade six, students must be aware of how these particular parts aid in the development of theme, setting, and plot. This foundational work in the earlier grades coalesces in grade seven with a grasp of how form and structure contribute to meaning. With this understanding in place, grade-eight students compare and contrast two or more texts and consider how different structures affect meaning and style. In grades nine and ten, students analyze how the author's choice of different text structures creates mystery, tension, or surprise. In the capstone experience in grades eleven and twelve, students analyze how the author's choices add to a text's structure and meaning as well as to the aesthetic impact of the overall work.

With informational text, kindergarten students merely need to identify the front and back covers and title page. Students in grades one through three attend to text features of both print and digital media (e.g., tables of contents, headings, bold words, glossaries, icons, and hyperlinks). In grades four and five, students consider text structures (e.g., chronology, compare and contrast, cause and effect, and problem and solution). Students in grades six through eight devote their energies to determining how component pieces of the text (e.g., sentence, paragraph, chapter, or section) work symbiotically to create coherence and meaning. Finally, students in grades eleven and twelve evaluate how authors use these components to develop the text's exposition or argument.

Text Type

Before students can begin breaking apart text, we first have to ensure that they are familiar with the major types of text, i.e., storybooks, poetry, and information. An easy way to initiate this discussion is by having students identify the front cover, back cover, and title page to learn the nature of the text. This proves significant in early literacy development because when young readers understand that books contain these types of texts, then they will develop a realistic sense of what they can expect to find within the pages of a book.

Materials

- Collection of books by text type (e.g., storybooks, poems, information books)

Directions

Bring in several examples of the text type you are teaching and read them with your students. As you do so, continue to reinforce the characteristics of this text type. When students become comfortable with this category, follow the same process with another text type (e.g., poetry). Before moving from these two text types, bring in new examples of the text types you've studied and ask students if they can identify the text type of each text based on its cover and the way the words are printed. Then move on to information books, adhering to the same progression.

Focus Questions

1. What kind of book is this? How do you know?
2. What is the difference between these two books? What makes each of them special?

● Book Sort

In the primary classroom, books abound . . . in libraries, book displays, take-home book bags, and so on. Students need to be able to recognize what types of books they see as well as to select the ones they want to read based on the category. A student who loves horses may simply want to read a story about them, while an information book may be more appropriate for a student who wants to learn more about horses. Understanding how to identify the difference between types of text allows students to enjoy the books they select, and this knowledge also empowers them to search actively for the kind of books they desire.

Materials

- A collection of books with different text types (e.g., storybooks, poems, information books)

Directions

Ask a small group of students to look at a selection of books and sort them into three categories: storybooks, poetry, and information. After students classify the texts, invite them to share how they identified which book belongs in which category. Counter any misunderstandings in discriminating between fiction and nonfiction by emphasizing that information books commonly contain tables of contents, headings, bold print, captions, glossaries, and indexes.

Focus Questions

1. What kind of book is this? How do you know?
2. Is this a storybook? How do you know?
3. Is this poetry? How do you know?
4. Is this an information book? How do you know?

Fiction Versus Nonfiction

Distinguishing between fiction and nonfiction enables young readers to anticipate what they will find in books as well as to frame their understanding of text. While the basic concept is relatively simple, students at this age have vivid imaginations and do not always grasp the difference between real and make-believe. To foster an awareness of the unique nature of fiction and nonfiction, we begin each new text by including an explicit statement about which type it is and explain how we know. At the end of the text, we review by asking students to tell us what kind of text it is and how they know, and eliciting specific details from the text to support their answers.

Materials

- Chart paper and marker

Directions

Introduce or review the definitions of "fiction" and "nonfiction." Remind students that fiction refers to imaginary stories created by an author. They did not really occur. On the other hand, nonfiction texts are about real people, places, and things. Nonfiction authors want readers to learn something from these texts. After your students become familiar with both text types, encourage them to become authors.

First, complete a guided nonfiction writing activity highlighting what has happened in school that day. Emphasize to your students that all of the things you are writing about actually happened. Then complete a guided fiction writing activity in which students list what they *wish* had happened in school that day (e.g., recess all day, pizza for lunch, no rules for anybody). This time, emphasize that these events come from students' imaginations.

Focus Questions

1. Is this book fiction or nonfiction? How do you know?
2. What is special about fiction?
3. What is special about nonfiction?

Story Pictures

Narrative structure in the primary grades tends to follow a predictable story grammar that can be particularly beneficial to struggling students. When students gain an awareness that stories inherently contain a beginning, middle, and end, and that these individual aspects work together to propel the story forward to a natural conclusion, it can greatly increase their comprehension.

Materials

- Stories with a strong sequence
- Writing and drawing materials

Directions

Discuss with students that stories (narratives) must have a beginning that starts the action, a middle that highlights the action and an ending that concludes the action. Model this concept by telling a personal story of something that happened over the past weekend (e.g., going to a museum, having dinner with friends, seeing a movie). Stop throughout the story to call students' attention to the different sections of the story. Then tell another story and ask students to identify the different sections of it, and to make illustrations that show the beginning, middle, and end.

As students gain proficiency, follow that activity with one in which they tell their own stories, explaining the beginning, middle, and end. Then encourage them to tell more stories, adding illustrations. Finally, move the storytelling to authentic texts. The chart below can provide students with a visual representation of narrative structure—both in their retelling of others' stories and in the creation of their own.

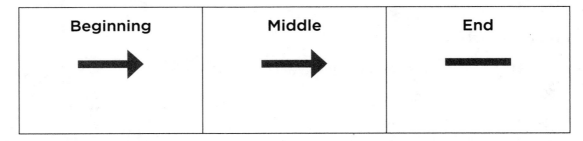

Beginning	Middle	End

Focus Questions

1. What are the three main parts of a story?

2. Why is the beginning of the story important? What if a story does not have a beginning? Why is the middle important? What happens to a story that doesn't have a middle? Why is the end important? Can we understand the story without it?

3. What happens at the beginning of this story?

4. What happens in the middle of this story?

5. What happens at the end of this story?

 Targeted Reading Interventions for the Common Core © 2014 by Diana Sisson & Betsy Sisson, Scholastic Teaching Resources

Where the Action Is

As young students develop story grammar and an understanding of the natural progression of narratives, they often fail to connect the beginning, middle, and end of a story. Struggling readers will often recount these three major phases of a narrative as disjointed events, randomly retelling what they can remember and omitting key events. We have found one of the easiest ways to highlight the connections among the beginning, middle, and end is to actually start with the middle—where the action is. From there, we demonstrate how the beginning introduces the action and the end concludes the action. By looking first at the middle (where most students can easily identify the action), we can start at a place where young readers have confidence and help them build the connections among the different temporal aspects of the action.

Materials and Preparation

- A narrative text that has a clear action sequence
- Chart paper and marker

Create a graphic like the one shown below.

Directions

Read the text with students. Then ask them what happened in the story. As students share their responses, fill in the center action bubble in the graphic. Next, ask students how the story begins. Keep their focus on how the action discussed in the middle of the story is introduced. Add the beginning action to the left bubble in the graphic. Then ask students how the story ends. Make certain that they again make a connection between the two action events. Add the ending action to the bubble on the right in the graphic. To ensure that your students can clearly see the direct links among the actions at different points in the story, retell the story using only the graphic.

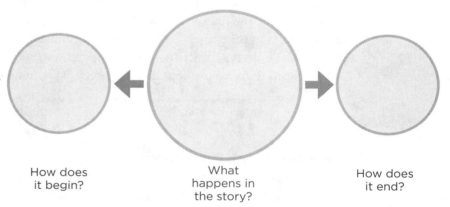

How does it begin? | What happens in the story? | How does it end?

Focus Questions

1. What happens in the story?
2. How does the action begin?
3. How does the action end?
4. Retell the story using only the graphic.

Tell Me a Story

Distinguishing among the sequential elements of a narrative's action proves difficult for most struggling readers—as well as many able readers. We find that we need to provide extensive scaffolding to help students understand the different time components of a story (beginning, middle, and end) and how the action of the story binds these components together to create a coherent narrative. We often begin with connecting the elements to students' own lives, moving to drawing pictures of the action sequence (see "Story Pictures" on page 74), then tying the action sequence to the middle events (see "Where the Action Is" on page 75), and finally moving to this writing activity, where they become responsible for making the bonds among the beginning, middle, and end apparent in their own writing.

Directions

After extensive modeling and guided practice with recognizing the beginning, middle, and end of a story, provide students with an action. Explain that this is the middle part of a story and that they will write a story around it. Direct them to decide how the action would start (beginning of the story). Then ask them to determine how the action will conclude (end of the story). As students write, reinforce that their beginning and end must connect to the middle action. After they finish their stories, have them read their work to others in the group. To further strengthen students' mastery of this skill, ask the audience if they can identify the beginning, middle, and end of the stories.

The Action Bank below contains some middle actions you might want to use.

Action Bank

Floppy, the bunny, is lost in the forest. *Where is her family? Will they find her?*

Jack, the wolf, falls into a hole. *What happens? Will he get out?*

Hank, the dog, discovers a red boot. *How does he find it? Will he return it to its owner?*

Kate and Nate are keeping a secret! *What is it? Will they tell anyone?*

Carlos and Liz go to a birthday party. *Whose party is it? What happens at the party?*

Kana and Mika go to a new school. *Why do they move? What happens on their first day?*

Connor enters a bike race. *Why does he enter? Does he win?*

Natasha loses her house keys. *How does she lose them? Will she get them back?*

Joel finds $20. *Where does he find it? Will he find the owner?*

Maria makes a new friend. *How does she meet her or him? What do they do together as friends?*

Focus Questions

1. How would this story begin? Does it match the action that happens in the middle of the story?

2. How would this story end? Does it match the action that happens in the beginning and middle of the story?

Targeted Reading Interventions for the Common Core © 2014 by Diana Sisson & Betsy Sisson, Scholastic Teaching Resources

Puzzle Pieces

Different types of text require different reading strategies. One of the characteristics of a struggling reader, however, is the failure to recognize that not all texts are the same. Text types have key structural elements that can furnish signposts to help guide struggling students as they read. For example, we know that stanzas in a poem function almost as paragraphs found in prose passages, and we can roughly equate these two elements to scenes in a drama.

Materials and Preparation

- A collection of stories, dramas, and poems
- Index cards and marker

Create a set of cards for each text type. Write one component of the text type on a separate card as shown at the right.

Story	Drama	Poem
Chapter/ Paragraph	Scene	Stanza
Sentence	Character dialogue	Line

Directions

Teach students about the parts of stories, dramas, and poems. Show samples of each type of text, and read texts that exemplify the components of each type. Mix up the cards and then place them on a table. Ask students to arrange the cards that should go together. When students finish, invite them to describe how they made their decisions.

Focus Questions

1. Which parts go together? Why?

2. What is the smallest part of each kind of text? How are sentences, character dialogue, and poetry lines similar to one another? How are they different?

3. When put together, what do these parts make? How are chapters/paragraphs, scenes, and stanzas similar to one another? How are they different?

4. When added together, what do these parts make? How are stories, dramas, and poems similar to one another? How are they different?

Extension Activities

* Instruct students to match the cards to text samples; for example, which text matches the Stanza card, the Scene card, the Chapter/Paragraph card?

* Encourage students to match the cards based on text length (i.e., Story/Drama/ Poem, Chapter/Paragraph/Scene/Stanza, Sentence/Character dialogue/Line). Discuss how each level is similar among the texts and how they serve to build on one another.

Literary Scavenger Hunt

Poetry, Drama, and Prose—after exposure and guided practice, students need to apply their new learning in a different context. In this activity, we ask students to use their understanding of text structure to locate examples in the world around them.

Materials and Preparation

- A collection of stories, poems, and dramas
- Chart paper and marker

Create a Comparison Chart: Stories Poems, Drama (see below).

Directions

Review the similarities and differences among the main types of text shown on the Comparison Chart: Stories, Poems, and Drama. Highlight for your students the unique structural elements of each one in the exemplar texts you've gathered. Then send them off on a scavenger hunt, using trade books, anthologies, and the classroom library to locate and identify as many examples as possible of the three text types.

COMPARISON CHART: STORIES, POEMS, DRAMA

TEXT TYPE	MAIN SECTIONS	MADE UP OF
Story	Chapter/Paragraph	Sentence
Poem	Stanza	Line
Drama	Scene	Character dialogue

Focus Questions

1. How do you know you are reading a story?

2. How can you recognize poems? In what ways are they different from stories?

3. How do you know that you are reading a play? What makes a play different from stories and poems?

Build-a-Poem

Understanding that poems have components including stanzas and lines is the first step in developing students' understanding of how literary forms function. The next step focuses on how these components work in tandem to develop the author's message, building on one another until they form a coherent telling.

Materials and Preparation

- A poem with at least three stanzas
- Scissors
- Paper clips

Type a copy of the poem, leaving extra space below each stanza. Make a copy of the poem for each student. Then cut apart the stanzas so students will have enough room to write below each stanza. Paperclip the stanzas together.

Directions

Give a set of stanzas to each student. Direct them to read each stanza and write down one sentence that summarizes it in the space below the stanza. Next, ask students to number the stanzas in the order they believe makes the most sense. Then have the group read the poem in its entirety, reflecting on the logical progression of its stanzas.

Focus Questions

1. Can you summarize this stanza? What does this stanza of the poem tell you about?

2. Which order makes the most sense for the stanzas to be in? Why?

3. What would happen if you moved the stanzas in a different order? Would it change the meaning of the poem? Would the poem still make sense? Why?

Drama Rewind

This activity stresses the significance of the cumulative nature of storytelling. The conventional approach to reading is through a linear progression from beginning to end. In contrast, this activity capitalizes on engaging students by reading backward, from the end to the beginning. This compels students to consider how narratives build in a logical progression of events and ideas as they reflect on what must have previously occurred to create the action they are reading about in a text.

Materials

- Readers Theater script

Directions

Select an appropriate reader's theater script for students. With no explanation of the plot, read the last scene first. Then lead a discussion about what happens in the scene. Guide students in making predictions about what must have happened previously in the play in order for this scene to take place. Read the scene prior to the last scene, and ask students to predict what happens in the previous scene. Continue with this process until you reach the first scene. Finish the activity by emphasizing that each scene is an individual part of the story but that each part builds on the previous one in the telling of the narrative. Remove one scene, or reorder them, and the narrative collapses.

Focus Questions

1. Summarize this scene. What has taken place?

2. What do you think must have happened before this scene? Use details from the text to support your answer.

3. Are your predictions correct? Use details from the text to support your answer.

4. Does the text make sense to you? What would happen if you removed one of the scenes? Use details from the text to support your answer.

5. What would happen if you moved the scenes to a different order? Would the story still make sense? Use details from the text to support your answer.

Targeted Reading Interventions for the Common Core © 2014 by Diana Sisson & Betsy Sisson, Scholastic Teaching Resources

CHAPTER 6

Point of View and Author's Purpose

Assess how point of view or purpose shapes the content and style of a text (CCSS, p. 10).

What students need to . . .

KNOW
- Point of view
- Author's purpose
- Content of text
- Style of text

UNDERSTAND
- The narrative point of view of a text affects both what is revealed in the story as well as how the story is told and what the reader takes away from the text.
- In informational text, the point of view influences the focus of the text as well as the information it provides.
- The content and style of the text is directly shaped by the author's purpose in writing the text.

DO
- Assess how point of view shapes the content and style of text.
- Assess how purpose shapes the content and style of text.

Pedagogical Foundations

CCR6 takes readers into a more intimate understanding of texts and authors' choices. It not only focuses on how authors develop texts but also on how the information they convey to their readers can be altered by a simple change of point of view. This, in turn, affects the content of a text as well as its presentation style, which ultimately impacts readers' ability to make meaning from text (Lyon, 1998; Molden, 2007; Sisson & Sisson, 2014). The author's purpose for writing a text is equally significant. It is vital that students grasp the author's purpose for writing a text (e.g., to inform, to instruct, to entertain, or to persuade). Each of these purposes is unique and distinctive and provides information to shape the reader's view of the content to fulfill the author's purpose (Ash, 2005; Davis, 1944; Fisher & Frey, 2012; Freebody & Luke, 1990; Meyer, 1987; Molden, 2007; Pardo, 2004; Paul & Elder, 2003). Thus, a reader who is aware that the purpose of a text is to persuade will be cognizant that only details that support the author's purpose will be included. Consequently, the reader may not be privy to all pertinent details and should not blindly accept the premises set out in the text.

●●●●●●●●●●●

Transitional Steps for Student Mastery

The initial step in acquiring skills for recognizing point of view begins in kindergarten where students must identify and define the roles of authors and illustrators. Grade-one students must be able to recognize who is telling the story they are reading. This solidifies in grade two when students identify the author's purpose and differentiate among differences in the points of view of characters. This understanding contrasts with students' own points of view in grade three. Comparing and contrasting different points of view found in multiple stories with a focus on first- and third-person narratives and firsthand and secondhand accounts takes place in grade four; in grade five, students become aware of how point of view affects how events are described. Grade-six students consider how authors develop points of view, while grade-seven students study how authors develop and contrast different points of view within a single text as well as how they differentiate their own points of view from those of others. Students in grade eight learn how these different points of view create textual effects, such as suspense or humor, and how authors can acknowledge and react to different points of view or evidence. Students in grades nine and ten analyze point of view through the lens of world literature and explore the use of rhetoric to support the author's point of view or purpose. Finally, in grades eleven and twelve, students analyze how points of view discriminate between explicit statements and implicit meanings, such as sarcasm, irony, and understatement. Within nonfiction, they consider how the author's point of view or purpose adds to the aesthetic nature and strength of the text.

You Be the Author

We begin each story we read to young children with a reminder of what an author does and what an illustrator does. Then we introduce the author and illustrator of the book. We also like to read the biographical sketches on the back flap to students. Conveying personal information about authors and illustrators humanizes them and makes them more interesting to students. It provides a great way for students to connect to authors and illustrators. For example, we talk about where the author and illustrator live in relation to us, if they have pets, and so on. After we finish reading the story, we bring students' attention back and ask simple questions: *Who is the author? Who wrote this story? Who is the illustrator? Who drew the pictures?* We also recommend you give your students a lot of authentic practice in learning how to be an author.

Materials

- Writing materials

Directions

Tell your students that today is a very special day. Today they will all be authors. Talk with students about what an author does and how anyone who has a story to tell can be an author. Then brainstorm possible subjects together. Using a guided writing format, create the story. Afterward, post the story in the classroom with students listed as co-authors.

Focus Questions

1. What does an author do?

2. Who is the author of this story?

3. What is interesting about the author's life?

You Be the Illustrator

The roles of illustrators and authors go hand in hand. We teach students these roles at the same time and emphasize that they are equally important. Each tells part of a story, and they work together to help us enjoy the text.

Materials

- Completed story from "You Be the Author" (p. 83)
- Drawing materials

Directions

This is a continuation of "You Be the Author" on the previous page. After students have shared their story in writing, tell them today they will be illustrators. Remind them that the pictures that illustrators draw must show us some part of the story and help us to understand better what is happening in it. Ask each student to draw a picture about something that happened in the story, a particular character, or another aspect. Make certain to provide time for students to share their illustrations and tell classmates what their pictures represent from the story. After everyone has shared his or her illustration, write the word *illustrator* on each drawing and post it by the original story.

Focus Questions

1. What does an illustrator do?
2. Who is the illustrator of this story?
3. What is interesting about the illustrator's life?

Everyone Can Tell a Story

Before students can grasp first-person or third-person narrations, as they will be expected to do in grade four, we need to begin helping them consider that someone is always telling a story. Sometimes that person is the author, and sometimes the author lets a character tell the story. The story changes if the author tells it, one character tells it, or several characters tell it. To demonstrate this, we read several examples of each of these possibilities, talking about how to recognize who is telling the story and how readers can learn different things based on who is telling the story during different parts of the action.

Materials

- A book with multiple narrators

Directions

After a shared event (e.g., lunch, recess), ask several students to tell what just happened. As they recount their stories, ask them who is talking and draw their attention to how the stories differ from one student to the next. Explain that this also happens in the stories that we read. Then read the book to your students. Pause frequently to ask students if they know who is telling the story.

Focus Questions

1. Who is telling the story? How do you know?
2. Is the author telling the story? How do you know?
3. Is a character telling the story? How do you know?
4. Is the same person telling the whole story? How do you know?
5. If someone new begins to tell the story, does this change the story? How?

● Look Who's Talking!

Primary students love hearing a story for the simple pleasure it brings them. While we want to maintain that love of literature, we also want to engage them in textual analysis—even at this young age. Rather than merely considering the story as a whole, we encourage students to think more deeply about what makes a good story. This activity asks students to reflect upon who is telling the story, why the author chose that character to tell it, and how the character selected to tell the story may change the way we understand it.

Materials

- A fictional story with a strong narrative

Directions

Read the story aloud to your students. Assign each student either the author or a character from the narrative. Give them time to draw a picture of the author or character. Now, reread the book slowly. Instruct students to listen carefully to who is telling the story. When they think the author is speaking, those students should hold up their picture of the author. When they think that a particular character is narrating the story, those students should hold up their picture of the relevant character. When the narrator changes, discuss with students how the reader knows that someone different is telling the story.

Focus Questions

1. Who is telling the story? How do you know?

2. Is the author telling the story? How do you know?

3. Is a character telling the story? How do you know?

4. Does the same person tell the entire story? How do you know?

5. If someone new begins to tell the story, does it change the story? How?

POV With Dialogue

Young readers begin to get a sense of point of view when an adult reader assumes different voices when reading aloud to them. We begin modeling how the voice we take on signifies how readers should relate to the character. Our voices should also match what we see represented in the pictures and what is happening in the story. Is the character excited? Sad? Scared? Curious? We direct students' attention to how voice helps us understand the story—and along the way, they begin to appreciate the role of point of view.

Materials

- A collection of fiction texts with diverse characters and rich dialogue
- A simplified Readers Theater script

Directions

Scaffold your students through this four-step process.

Step 1: Begin by discussing what point of view is, providing examples from home and school with an emphasis on how each student's point of view may be different from other students or from their parents.

Step 2: Read your selection of texts. Emphasize the differing voices and how each person's point of view in the story shows that person's feelings and thoughts and adds to our understanding of the story.

Step 3: Next, introduce the Readers Theater script. Ask each student to take a role and practice how his or her character's voice might sound, and why.

Step 4: Finally, have students write their own story, complete with dialogue. Work one-on-one with students to craft their stories, their characters' points of view, and how their voices represent who they are in the story.

Complete the project by having students present their stories, followed by a group discussion of why others believe that the characters had the voices they did, as well as how their points of view differ from those of other characters.

Focus Questions

1. What is point of view?

2. Is your point of view different from other people's (e.g., parents, friends, and your teacher)? Why?

3. How does this character sound? Why does he or she sound like this?

4. What point of view does this character have? Why do you think that is his or her point of view?

Who Am I?

We believe that the best way for students to learn is through engagement with the content. In other words, to learn, they have to do. So, if we want students to understand how voice reflects character, they need to try using voices themselves. This fun activity lets students do just that.

Materials

- A story with engaging characters and dialogue
- Sentence strips
- Marker

Directions

After reading the story with your students, write one line of dialogue on a sentence strip for each student, detailing which characters they are. Allow time for students to practice how to read the dialogue. After students have practiced, ask them to read their dialogue in the voice they imagine the character would use. The other students have to guess who the character is and explain how the voice helped them make the identification.

Focus Questions

1. Who is speaking? How do you know?

2. How does the voice help you know which character is speaking?

Character Masks

Taking on the voice of a character may seem like a relatively unsophisticated task for students; however, this is a precursor to their ability to analyze a character. In order to determine an appropriate voice, the reader must first identify key details about the character and then translate that into an oral representation. Making a character mask offers another step in this process by encouraging students to focus first on the visual elements of a character and then on how such a character might sound if brought to life.

Materials

- A story with a strong main character
- Sheets of construction paper in different colors
- Crayons and markers
- Scissors
- Tape
- String

Directions

Read the story with students. Then have each student create a mask for one of the characters in the story. Guide students' thinking as they work to help them consider how their character mask should appear based on textual details. Transition this into a discussion about how the character would sound (e.g., old, funny, angry, happy). Invite students to don their masks and recount the story using their voices to project the character.

Focus Questions

1. What is point of view?
2. What does the character look like? Use details from the text to create your mask.
3. What does your character sound like? Use details from the text to help you.

Narrator POV

Struggling students often fail to grasp the concept that narrators tell stories from different points of view, and that this affects the story being told. Taking on the role of narrator creates authenticity, real-world understanding, and . . . a little bit of fun!

Materials

- A wordless picture book for each student
- Writing materials

Directions

After giving each student a different wordless picture book, remind students that a narrator is the person who tells the story. Instruct them to write a story that matches the illustrations in their book. Next, ask each student to become the narrator and read their text to their classmates. Discuss with them how their stories contrast and how different narrators bring different points of view to the story.

Focus Questions

1. What is point of view?
2. What is a narrator? What does he or she do?
3. Who is telling this story?
4. Does the story change based on the narrator telling the story? How?

Character Sketch

We encourage students to connect to what they read, but we do not want to let their own background knowledge and personal feelings cause them to misunderstand a text's meaning. Students need to distinguish their own point of view from that of the book and be objective in how they construct meaning.

Materials

- A narrative text
- Writing materials

Directions

After reading the narrative, ask students to write a brief character sketch in which they describe what the main character looks like, says, does, thinks, and feels. Afterward, have each student trade his or her sketch with a partner. The partner's task is to look in the text and verify that there is evidence for each character statement. If evidence exists, they check off the statement. If they can't find any evidence to support the statement, they circle it. As soon as students complete their verification, lead a discussion about the circled items. If there is no evidence to support certain statements, question what prompted students to voice that opinion. Throughout the lesson, emphasize that readers have to separate their own point of view (POV) from that of the story. If not, the reader may come away with a false sense of what the author is trying to communicate.

Focus Questions

1. What is point of view?

2. Who is telling this story?

3. What is your point of view about the story? Is it different from the author's? Is it the same? Does your point of view change the story?

It's All in the Eye of the Beholder

We want students taking on the role of author as much as possible. Why? Beyond the obvious benefits of developing their literary skills, becoming authors provides an authentic context for students to master key reading skills. Thus, if students are to be capable of differentiating their own point of view from that of the narrator or characters, then asking them to tell one story from multiple points of view will cultivate this skill.

Materials

- A story
- Writing materials

Directions

After reading a story, create a storytelling circle. Direct the first student to retell the story through the point of view of the narrator as it was originally related to readers. Other students continue to retell the story—from different characters' points of view. Each student explains how their character's point of view would change as the story unfolds. For example, in the story of Cinderella, the first student would retell the story as it is traditionally told—through the point of view of the title character. Other students would retell the story through the point of view of the stepmother, the stepsisters, the fairy godmother, and the prince. For example, how would the stepmother view Cinderella working in the castle? Not attending the ball? Meeting the prince? Marrying the prince? Considering the story through these very different viewpoints significantly alters the narrative as well as students' understanding of it and the impact of point of view in storytelling.

From this initial experience, ask students to write their own original story, following the same model. After a student shares his or her original story, encourage other students to retell the story through the point of view of other characters in that story.

If students find retelling the story through a different character's point of view too difficult, focus on one main event at a time. For example, rather than the entire story, focus on how each character would view Cinderella's appearance at the ball. How would the stepmother and stepsisters react? The fairy godmother? The prince?

Focus Questions

1. What is point of view?

2. Who is telling this story?

3. What is this character's point of view of the story? Is it different from the author's? Is it the same? Does your point of view change the story?

Targeted Reading Interventions for the Common Core © 2014 by Diana Sisson & Betsy Sisson, Scholastic Teaching Resources

CHAPTER 7

Diverse Text Formats and Media

Integrate and evaluate content presented in diverse media and formats, including visually and quantitatively, as well as in words (CCSS, p. 10).

What students need to . . .

KNOW

- Illustration
- Diagram
- Diverse media and formats

UNDERSTAND

- Illustrations and words work together to convey the story or message of a text.
- Multimedia formats share a common purpose in communicating an author's work but differ in how they are presented and ultimately interpreted by the viewer.

DO

- Use information gleaned from illustrations and text to construct meaning.
- Evaluate content in diverse media and formats, visually, quantitatively, and in words.

Pedagogical Foundations

CCR7 promotes students' appreciation of not only the written word in both traditional and digital media but also familiarizes them with the beauty of the theater and visual arts. To become educated citizens in the modern world, children need to recognize how varied media function together symbiotically and serve multiple purposes with one common goal of presenting the author's ideas (Bus & Neuman, 2009; Ciampa, 2012; Coiro, 2003; Coiro, Knobel, Lankshear, & Leu, 2008; Goetz & Walker, 2004; Leu, 2000; Pantaleo, 2005; Rouet, Lowe, & Schnotz, 2008; Sisson & Sisson, 2014). It is imperative that students grasp how each text format and medium works within its own confines, has its own strengths and weaknesses, and how they collectively provide a more comprehensive picture of the author's message than any one single aspect can ever achieve.

●●●●●●●●●●●

Transitional Steps for Student Mastery

Students first begin recognizing diverse text formats and media in kindergarten when they look at the relationship between illustrations and text. In grade one, students use illustrations and textual details to describe the narrative elements of stories. By grade two, students use illustrations and text to show their understanding of these narrative elements as well as how they contribute to and clarify informational text. Students in grade three take a keener look at the inherent power of illustrations to enhance text, with students in grade four making connections between the usage of text and illustrations to tell stories. Grade-five students build on the work of the earlier grades to consider how visual and multimedia elements add to the meaning, tone, and/or beauty of a text. Meanwhile, students in grades three through five also begin to use and interpret illustrations found in nonfiction texts (e.g., maps, charts, diagrams, photographs, timelines, animations, and interactive elements in digital media). Students in grades six through eight focus on comparing and contrasting the experiences of reading, listening, and viewing texts. For example, in grade six they compare and contrast the experiences of what readers "see" and "hear" when reading a text to what they perceive that they "see" and "hear" when listening or watching. In grade seven the focus is on the effects of camera angles, stage lighting, and other techniques specific to particular artistic mediums. Grade eight then draws upon the skill set developed in middle school to consider the degree to which a production remains faithful to the original text and to evaluate the director's or actors' choices within those productions. Students in grades nine and ten build upon these skills by analyzing how subjects are treated in different artistic mediums, and students in grades eleven and twelve study how multiple interpretations reflect a single source as well as evaluate multiple informational sources across differing media formats.

Moment-by-Moment Action

Developing the cognitive skills to fathom the relationship between text and illustrations begins with personal connections. Before directing students' attention to the illustrations in a text, encourage them to construct their own mental images.

Materials
- A text that contains detailed description of the plot's action
- Drawing materials

Directions
Read aloud the text you've chosen. Stop periodically, and ask students to close their eyes and picture what is happening in the story at that moment. After discussing what images students see, provide time for them to create drawings that depict what they heard. Continue this process throughout the whole book. Finish by asking students if they can now retell the story using only their drawings to remind them of story events.

Focus Questions
1. What has just happened in the story?
2. What picture do you have in your mind right now? What did you hear that made you think of this?
3. Use your pictures to retell the story.

Time Freeze

After students are cognizant of the relationship between text and illustrations in a broad sense, they must next learn that illustrations present a picture in time that links to a particular piece of text. This insight will serve struggling readers when they encounter text beyond their normal reach.

Materials
- A picture book

Directions
Complete a picture walk with your students before reading the text. At each illustration, stop and talk about what the picture shows. Then tell students to listen carefully as you read the story. When they hear something that refers to what is happening in the picture, ask them to give a thumbs-up. Stop at that point, and ask what moment from the story is shown in the picture. Continue through the book using this format.

Focus Questions
1. What do you see in the picture?
2. When does the picture match the story?
3. What is happening in the story? In the picture?

Story Clues

We use guided prompts to mold students' understanding of the relationship between words and illustrations. For young readers, it is not enough to look at each one separately. We need to make explicit how the two aspects of text work in tandem. One way to do that is to focus first on illustration, then text, and finally to ask students what we now know as readers. This sequence forms the basis of their approach to text and how they go about making meaning while also enhancing their appreciation of text and illustrations.

Directions

When you read a picture book, use the following scaffold to guide students toward the understanding that pictures and words work together to provide clues about the text, specifically about characters, setting, and plot.

ILLUSTRATIONS	TEXT	WHAT DO WE KNOW?
What do you see in the pictures about the character? What does the character look like? What is the character doing? Is there anyone or anything else in the picture with the character?	How does the character look? What does the character say? What does the character think? What does the character feel? What do other characters say about the character?	How would you describe the character? Why do you think that? What clues did you use from the pictures or the story?
What do you see in the pictures about the setting? Where does the story take place? When does the story take place?	Do the words tell you where the story takes place? Are there any clues? Do the words tell you when the story takes place? Are there any clues?	What is the setting of the story? Why do you think that? What clues did you use from the pictures or the story?
What action is happening in the pictures?	What happens at the beginning of the story? In the middle? At the end? How is the problem resolved?	What are the main events of the story? Why do you think that? What clues did you use from the pictures or story?

Focus Questions

1. What do the pictures show?

2. What does the text tell the reader?

3. How do the pictures and the text work together to share the author's message?

4. How do the pictures and text help you understand the author's message?

5. Would the author's message be affected if there were no pictures? No text? Why?

Match Up

In early literacy, picture clues play a significant role in interpreting texts. Later, readers will use these clues to enhance their reading. The first step, however, is for them to realize that illustrations link to text. What better way to do this than for students to create their own pictures?

Materials

- A narrative text

Directions

After reading a story, ask each student to draw a picture of a different aspect of the text (e.g., character, setting, event). Remind them to add specific details. For example, when students draw the setting, ask them to include when the story takes place (e.g., day or night, season, a long time ago or happening now) and where it takes place (e.g., inside, outside, a specific place). When students are finished, ask them to share their pictures. As they do, be sure to highlight which aspects of the text you see reflected in their work.

Focus Questions

1. What do you see in the picture?
2. Does this picture show how the story describes it? How?
3. Can you tell part of the story just by looking at the picture?

Who Needs Words?

We have found an excellent strategy to guarantee that students employ illustrations as part of their meaning-making process. It simply requires wordless books and lots of talking about illustrations. With no words and no commentary from adults, students take the initiative to create their own narratives. Afterward, we like to go back to this visual "text" to help students turn their mental images into concrete understandings of character, setting, and events. Simple . . . but effective!

Materials

- A wordless picture book

Directions

Go through the book once, encouraging your students to tell the story they see unfolding. Then ask students to look at just the characters in the book and to describe them. Repeat the process for the setting and then the main events of the story.

Focus Questions

1. Who are the characters in the story? How would you describe them? How do the pictures help you describe them?
2. What is the setting of the story? When does it happen? Where does it happen? How do the pictures help you describe the setting?
3. What happens in the story? What happens first? Where do you see that in the pictures? What happens next? Where is that in the book? How does the story end? How do you know? How do the pictures help you understand what happens in the story?

Stop 'n' Go

Words and illustrations function as a collective text. Able readers understand that each supports the other as well as providing its own unique information about the story. This principle can be missing from the comprehension toolkits of struggling students.

Materials

- A big book

Directions

Young children love a game. Stop 'n' Go is an easy game that will motivate your students to attend to the text as well as the illustrations. Explain that you are going to stop throughout the story as you read it. When you do, you will say, "Stop." Ask students to find the part of the picture that you just described and then say, "Go."

Focus Questions

1. Where is the character? It says the character is _____. Where do you see that in the pictures?

2. When does the story take place? Does the picture show that?

3. Where is the story taking place? What pictures show that?

4. _____ just happened. Where is that in the pictures?

 Targeted Reading Interventions for the Common Core © 2014 by Diana Sisson & Betsy Sisson, Scholastic Teaching Resources

Treasure Hunt

Working backward can often furnish not only a different view of something but also a different understanding. We find that providing struggling students the "answers" and asking them to find the "questions" can be very helpful.

Materials

- A narrative text

Directions

After reading a story with your students, tell them that they are going on a treasure hunt. You will tell them something about the story, and they have to find it in the text—both in words and pictures. Students will share where they found their "treasure" with others and find out if other students found different places where that treasure is hidden.

Focus Questions

1. The main character is _____ . Where is the character described in the story?

2. The setting of the story is _____. It takes place during _____. It takes place at _____. Where is that in the story?

3. This happens in the story: _____. This happens first. This happens next. This happens at the end. Where do you find that in the book?

4. The problem in the story is _____. Which words tell you that? Which pictures show the problem?

5. The solution in the story is _____. Where do you find the solution?

Text and Pix

Struggling students often become frustrated and overwhelmed by the volume of words on a page. Using a sentence strip chunks the reading and lessens the amount of cognitive resources needed to link text to illustrations. It also allows students to manipulate text in a flexible context through which they can experiment and learn from their choices.

Materials and Preparation

- A text
- Sentence strips
- Marker
- Sticky notes
- Scissors

Write sentences from a text on sentence strips.

Directions

Give students the sentence strips and the accompanying book with the text covered with sticky notes. Instruct students to read the sentence strips and match them to the appropriate illustrations.

Focus Questions

1. What is happening in the picture?

2. Which picture matches the sentence strip? How do you know?

Text + Illustrations = Meaning

An important fix-up strategy for struggling readers is looking at visual elements to support textual understanding. Some students learn this coping technique early; however, many fail to utilize it to its fullest potential. They rely heavily on illustrations to construct meaning, but their comprehension can increase even more if they fully grasp the ways in which text and illustrations work in tandem to convey meaning. We encourage students to use text + illustrations = meaning as a formula for reading success. If they can't construct meaning, go back to the formula. Reread the text. Look again at the illustrations. Examine the text and the illustration together. Utilizing these two components offers students a framework for repairing comprehension and encourages them to be independent, active readers.

Materials

- A text
- Wikki Stix®

Directions

After reading the text with students, instruct them to look at the illustrations on each page and then at the words on the page. Explain to them that the words and the illustrations work together to help readers make meaning. Take the words or the pictures out, and readers lose part of what the author wants them to understand. Next, give students Wikki Stix and tell them to place the Wikki Stix under any words or phrases that talk about what they see in the illustrations. As they search for text-illustration links, guide students in a discussion about how the illustrations reflect what is happening in the text and how they differ from it. Focus on how the illustrations help them understand the text better.

Focus Questions

1. What do you see in the illustration?

2. Look at the text. Which words talk about what you see in the illustration?

3. How are the words and the illustrations different? Use details from the text to support your answer.

4. How are the words and the illustrations similar? Use details from the text to support your answer.

5. How does the illustration help you understand what is in the text?

 Targeted Reading Interventions for the Common Core © 2014 by Diana Sisson & Betsy Sisson, Scholastic Teaching Resources

Mood Elements

Beyond their importance in conveying the meaning of a text, illustrations also serve to build readers' appreciation of more advanced literary elements. Struggling readers who become frustrated with text should be encouraged to use picture clues to aid them in their understanding. Illustrations are particularly important in the development of mood. In this activity, we focus students' attention on five strategic features of mood, i.e., color, background, patterns, facial expressions, and body language.

Materials

- A picture book with illustrations that convey the features of mood

Directions

Read the book. Afterward, direct your students' attention to the illustrations and guide them through the features of mood expressed in the chart below.

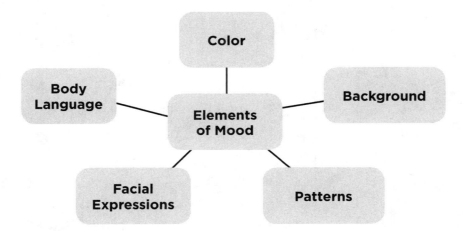

Focus Questions

1. Are the colors bright or are they dark? Which colors do you see the most? How do the colors make you feel?

2. What background do you see? Is it gloomy? Is there a sun?

3. Are any patterns present? Are they geometric, like circles and squares? Are they natural, like ivy or clouds? Are the shapes touching, or are they set apart? How does the pattern make you feel?

4. What facial expressions do you see? Do the characters look happy, sad, excited, confused?

5. What body language do the characters show? Are they standing up straight and confident? Are they slouching?

CHAPTER 8

Evaluate Arguments in Nonfiction Text

> *Delineate and evaluate the argument and specific claims in a text, including the validity of the reasoning as well as the relevance and sufficiency of the evidence* (CCSS, p. 10).

What students need to . . .

KNOW

- Argument
- Specific claims in text
- Validity of the reasoning
- Relevance and sufficiency of the evidence

UNDERSTAND

- Authors use specific reasons and evidence to support claims in texts.
- Readers must verify that the reasons authors use are valid and rational.
- Readers must determine if there is sufficient evidence to support author claims.

DO

- Delineate the argument and specific claims in a text.
- Evaluate the argument and specific claims in a text.

Targeted Reading Interventions for the Common Core © 2014 by Diana Sisson & Betsy Sisson, Scholastic Teaching Resources

Pedagogical Foundations

With an eye toward the need for readers to be able to identify supporting details in order to create strong main ideas and authorial points, CCR8 requires students to evaluate arguments in a text. Eventually, students need to use these skills as a means to assess a writer's skill in creating arguments and providing valid reasoning and evidence to support his or her claims (Fulton & Poeltler, 2013; Gomez-Zwiep & Harris, 2010; Griffith & Ruan, 2005; Nussbaum, 2008; Ogle & Blachowicz, 2002; Stobaugh, 2013). These foundational skills build students' abilities to read text with an awareness of not only what is necessary for a writer to build an argument but also with an understanding of what makes effective arguments. In turn, students utilize these skills to become thoughtful readers who reflect on a text's validity and reliability.

●●●●●●●●●●●

Transitional Steps for Student Mastery

There are no transitional steps in literature. This standard only applies to informational text because, with this type of text, students focus on how to evaluate arguments posed by authors. In kindergarten through grade one, students simply identify the overt reasons given by an author to support the points made in the text. By grade two, students begin to consider the "how" of using reasons to support the author's points. The grade-three curriculum makes a significant leap in having students analyze arguments by focusing on text structure (e.g., comparison, sequence, cause/effect). Students in grades four and five build on this understanding to explain how authors use reasons and evidence to support their points. Sixth grade marks another rise in expectation. For the first time, students are asked to evaluate an author's argument and differentiate between points supported by reasons and evidence and those that are not. In grades seven through ten, with increasing sophistication, students assess the quality of the reasons and evidence. Is the reasoning sound? Does the evidence appear sufficient to support the claims? This culminates in eleventh and twelfth grade, when students utilize their skills to evaluate arguments made in seminal U.S. documents.

● That's Why

Before young students can understand how an author uses reasons to support his or her points, they must first make a more personal connection to their own lives. They can then use that understanding to bridge to authentic text.

Directions

Ask students questions about themselves, such as the ones in the Question Bank at right. As they share, ask them to explain their responses. Reinforce the idea that they must have reasons for their answers.

> **QUESTION BANK**
>
> What is your favorite book?
>
> What is your favorite food?
>
> What is your favorite holiday?
>
> What is your favorite movie?
>
> What is your favorite toy?

Focus Questions

1. Why do you feel that way?
2. What reasons do you have for saying that?

● Because the Author Said So

Becoming a critical reader begins in the primary grades, when students are asked to identify the reasons an author provides to support his or her ideas. In later grades, we expect students to evaluate those reasons, but for now, we focus solely on students' ability to locate them.

Materials

- An informational text

Directions

Read the text you selected to your students. After discussing the text, read it again. This time, explain that you will stop several times. When you reach these stopping points, ask, "Why does the author say . . . ?" Model the process first and then provide explicit, guided practice.

Focus Questions

1. Why does the author say . . . ?
2. What reasons does the author give for saying this?

● Just Because

We like to familiarize struggling students with easy strategies that help them be as independent as possible. The word *because* is an excellent example of this, as it commonly marks when something is about to be explained. While we cannot guarantee that the word will appear in all of the text students read, it does add a valuable strategy to their reading toolkit!

Materials and Preparation

- An informational text with cause-and-effect structure that features the word *because*
- Pencils
- Chart paper and marker or interactive whiteboard

Make a copy of the text, or a portion of it, for each student. Create a display copy of the diagram shown below.

Directions

Model for your students how the word *because* functions as a signal that something is going to be explained. Display the diagram below to illustrate the principle. Explain to students that when they see the word *because,* the words after it explain the reasons the author gives about an idea or an event. As you begin reading the text, instruct your students to circle the word *because* every time they see it. As they do, stop and guide them in identifying the author's idea or event and the corresponding reasons.

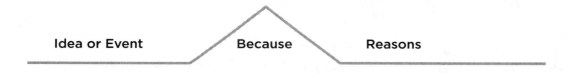

Idea or Event   **Because**   **Reasons**

Focus Questions

1. The author says _____. Why does he or she say that?

2. What reasons does the author give?

Reading TPR

We have always believed that students learn by doing. Using Total Physical Response (TPR) activities in which we engage students' bodies in the learning process is one way that we do this. TPR is obviously a source of engagement for young students, but it also helps cement their understanding of abstract concepts. In this strategy, we ask students to move when they hear a signal word and then to hold up their fingers as they identify reasons that provide evidence.

Materials and Preparation

- A nonfiction text that contains an argument
- An index card for each student
- A marker
- Short informational passage with a cause-and-effect structure that features the word *because*

Draw a question mark on each index card.

Directions

Review with your students how the word *because* signals when an author is going to give reasons for what he or she is explaining. See the "Just Because" strategy (page 105) for further explanation. Give each student an index card with a question mark on it. Explain that you are going to read a passage aloud, and each time they hear you read the word *because*, they should hold up their index card. Then, as you slowly read the passage after the word *because*, they should put up one finger if they hear a single reason, then another finger if they hear a second reason, and so on.

Focus Questions

1. The author says, _____. What reasons does he or she give to help you understand that?

2. What word helped you find the reasons?

Why Do You Say That?

For us, Vygotsky's Zone of Proximal Development (1962, 1978) drives the strategies that we devise for students. It is always important to scaffold students' learning from what they cannot do independently, to what they can do with guided support, to what they can accomplish on their own. With a struggling reader, this scaffolding is essential. These students regularly face academic situations in which they become frustrated and lack the necessary skills to succeed, so it is our job to give them opportunities to understand and excel with content. That means that we look initially for ways to make real-life connections that students understand and then slowly transition them to independence through skill building and guided practice. This strategy provides that real-life connection without the anxiety of reading and trying to comprehend text. Understand the concept—then apply the concept to text. That is our rule!

Directions

Before approaching text, work with your students to understand how authors use reasons to support their points. The easiest way to do this is to bring the concept into their personal lives. Talk about how everything in life has a reason: When someone says something, they have a reason for saying it. Give a kid-friendly example, such as this one: *Think about homework. You have homework every night. Is there a reason for that? Why do you think teachers give homework? We do it because it helps you learn. You have time to practice what you learn in class. Also, when you bring back your homework, we can see if you understand everything or if we need to give you some extra help.* After this discussion, ask students if they can give you reasons for some particular points (such as the examples below).

> You need to go to bed early.
>
> You may not run in the hallways.
>
> You need to raise your hand before you speak in class.
>
> You should look both ways before you cross the street.
>
> You should eat lots of vegetables and fruits.

Focus Questions

1. What reasons do you hear?

2. Why are reasons important?

You Decide!

We emphasize the reading-writing connection in all the work that we do. If you want students to internalize learning and "own" it, they need to write. Why? Because if they can express their thinking, then they truly understand the content. That is the goal of every strategy!

Directions

It is always helpful to put students in the place of an author. What better way to understand the skills necessary to write a text than to have students use those skills themselves? Tell your students that they are going to practice giving reasons for their ideas—just like the authors that they read. Model the first prompt shown below, and then ask students to answer the succeeding prompts. As students share their reasons, offer reinforcements to show that their reasons are explicit and clearly related to the prompt.

My favorite food is _____ because _____ .

My favorite holiday is _____ because _____ .

My favorite subject is _____ because _____ .

My favorite movie is _____ because _____ .

My favorite book is _____ because _____ .

Focus Questions

1. What are your reasons?

2. Are your reasons clear?

3. Do your reasons match the prompt?

Extension Activity

∗ You may change this from an oral activity to a writing activity, depending on the skill level of your students.

Musical Text

As students enter the intermediate grades, we expect that they will move from identifying reasons that authors provide to analyzing how authors arrange these reasons. Developing this skill helps students better understand an author's points better as well as incorporate this knowledge into their own writing.

Materials

- Text Structure Word Bank (p. 110) for each student
- Writing materials
- Background music

Directions

Explain that authors use text structures as a way to present their reasons to readers. For instance, they may use main idea to present an idea and then use details to explain their reasons. They may choose sequence and list their reasons one at a time. They may compare and contrast reasons or show reasons as the cause in a cause-and-effect structure.

Designate each student as an "expert" in one of the text structures found in paragraphs, e.g., main idea, sequence, compare and contrast, and cause and effect. Then give each student a topic on which to write. While music is playing in the classroom, have students write about their topic, following the text structure in which they are an expert. (Encourage them to use the Text Structure Word Bank reproducible to aid them in their writing.) When the music stops, they pass their paper to another student. That student then writes to that topic—again following the text structure in which they are an expert. The process continues until everyone has written on each of the topics.

Afterward, ask your students to read the paper they have in their hands. As they read, challenge the other students to identify the different text structures.

Focus Questions

1. How does the author arrange these sentences? How can you tell?

2. How is each structure different?

Name_____ Date _____

TEXT STRUCTURE WORD BANK

TEXT STRUCTURE	SIGNAL WORDS	
Main Idea	one reason	mainly
	another reason	most important
	for example	sums up
Sequence	first	after
	second	before
	next	earlier
	later	following
	finally	then
	last	while
Compare and Contrast	like	as well as
	unlike	much as
	different from	similarly
	same as	however
	alike	on the other hand
	instead	yet
	but	though
Cause and Effect	because	for this reason
	since	if . . . then
	as a result	not only . . . but also

 Targeted Reading Interventions for the Common Core © 2014 by Diana Sisson & Betsy Sisson, Scholastic Teaching Resources

Compare-and-Contrast Signposts

Visual representations offer struggling students a tangible means upon which to draw when they encounter unfamiliar content. In the case of evaluating the logical progression of an author's ideas (e.g., compare and contrast, cause and effect, or sequence), signal words function as "signposts," alerting students as to what to expect from the text as well as how to approach and make meaning from it.

Materials

- Signal Words: Compare and Contrast (p. 112) for each student

- A copy of a compare and contrast text that contains numerous signal words for each student

- Pencils

Directions

Teach students the signal words for compare and contrast text on the reproducible. Then give them a compare and contrast text that contains several of those signal words. Ask students to circle the signal words and explain how each one signals that the author is comparing or contrasting something.

Focus Questions

1. Which words tell you that this passage is comparing and contrasting something? Use details from the text to support your answer.

2. What is the author comparing and contrasting? Use details from the text to support your answer.

Name_____ Date _____

SIGNAL WORDS: COMPARE AND CONTRAST

like	unlike	resemble	different from
same as	compared	alike	similar
alternatively	apart from	by contrast	contrary to
instead	conversely	despite	even though
however	but	nonetheless	on the other hand
otherwise	rather	except	other than

Targeted Reading Interventions for the Common Core © 2014 by Diana Sisson & Betsy Sisson, Scholastic Teaching Resources

Cause-and-Effect Signposts

Cause-and-effect patterns often baffle students, who complain that they cannot distinguish between the two. Recognizing the signal words inherent in this pattern provides one structure. Unfortunately, students can rarely separate the two because they do not appear linearly in the texts they read. For example, students expect to see that the cause will precede the effect. Text, however, does not always adhere to this structural design. Consequently, we first teach students the signal words that function as signposts in their reading, but we add directional signals so that struggling readers will know where to look for cause and effect in the text.

Materials

- Signal Words: Cause and Effect (p. 114) for each student
- A text with a cause-and-effect structure that contains numerous signal words for each student

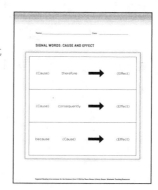

Directions

Teach students the signal words commonly used to indicate cause and effect, shown on the reproducible, using the arrow to indicate the logical flow from cause to effect. Then instruct students to read a text that contains cause-and-effect sentences or paragraphs, circle the signal words, write a "C" above the text that illustrates the cause, write an "E" above the text that reflects the effects of the causes, and draw an arrow toward the effect to demonstrate the natural progression of ideas. A sample is shown below.

Focus Questions

1. What is the signal word(s)?

2. What is the cause listed by the author? Use details from the text to support your answer.

3. What is the effect of that cause(s)? Use details from the text to support your answer.

Name_____ Date _____

SIGNAL WORDS: CAUSE AND EFFECT

(Cause)   therefore   ➡   (Effect)

(Cause)   consequently   ➡   (Effect)

because   (Cause)   ➡   (Effect)

Targeted Reading Interventions for the Common Core © 2014 by Diana Sisson & Betsy Sisson, Scholastic Teaching Resources

Sequencing Signposts

Sequencing ideas can be deceptively difficult. The key events or ideas appear to follow a logical order; however, without understanding the signal words found in sequential text patterns, students can falter in their understanding of text.

Materials

- Signal Words: Sequencing (p. 116) for each student

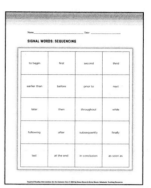

Directions

Teach the signal words for sequencing shown on the reproducible. Invite students to share (orally or in writing) how to do something in a sequential process (e.g., how to make a peanut butter and jelly sandwich, how to ride a bike, how to play a game). Emphasize that they must use their signal words to explain the natural order in which each step takes place.

Focus Questions

1. What is the signal word?

2. What happens at the beginning? What is your signpost to know that?

3. What happens next? What is your signpost to know that?

4. What happens at the end? What is your signpost to know that?

SIGNAL WORDS: SEQUENCING

to begin	first	second	third
earlier than	before	prior to	next
later	then	throughout	while
following	after	subsequently	finally
last	at the end	in conclusion	as soon as

Targeted Reading Interventions for the Common Core © 2014 by Diana Sisson & Betsy Sisson, Scholastic Teaching Resources

CHAPTER 9

Comparing and Contrasting Multiple Texts

Analyze how two or more texts address similar themes or topics in order to build knowledge or to compare the approaches the authors take (CCSS, p. 10).

What students need to . . .

KNOW

- Themes/topics
- Authors' approaches

UNDERSTAND

- Reading multiple texts on similar themes or topics builds a reader's background knowledge of the subject matter.

- Authors address similar themes or topics through diverse approaches that allow the reader to experience the subject matter in unique ways.

DO

- Analyze how two or more texts address similar themes or topics in order to build knowledge.

- Analyze how two or more texts address similar themes or topics and compare the approaches the authors take.

Pedagogical Foundations

CCR9 encourages students to visualize, articulate, and ultimately appreciate the universality of literature and our collective human need to express ourselves through storytelling as well as to take advantage of multiple informational texts as a means to enhance their learning on a given topic (Afflerbach & Cho, 2009; Bråten, Britt, Strømsø & Rouet, 2011; Duke, 2007; Heisey & Kucan, 2010; Moss, 2011; Neuman & Roskos, 2012; Voss & Wiley, 2000). An underlying theme in this standard is also the commonalities of how authors express themselves throughout a rich history of time periods and cultural backgrounds. In a world of ever-shrinking cultural boundaries, comparing and contrasting multiple texts allows students to view the world through a more intimate lens and to observe what makes us more alike than different (Colby & Lyon, 2004; Ebe, 2010; Kruse, 2001; Kuzminski, 2002; Louie, 2011; Taylor, 2000).

●●●●●●●●●●●

Transitional Steps for Student Mastery

Students in kindergarten and grade one focus on comparing and contrasting characters and experiences in stories. In kindergarten, emphasis is given to characters in familiar stories, and in grade one, more attention is given to the experiences of the characters. In grade two, students look at multiple versions of the same story, for example, the number of Cinderella stories from countries spanning the globe. Story elements—theme, setting, and plot—become the focus in grades three through five, with book series highlighted in grade three, stories, myths, and traditional literature from different cultures in grade four, and stories from a single genre in grade five. The grade-six curriculum emphasizes comparing and contrasting genres, while in grade seven, students compare and contrast a fictional portrayal of historical accounts. Students in grade eight attend to how modern works of fiction draw on themes, patterns of events, and character types derived from traditional texts, such as mythology, traditional tales, and religious works. This focus continues in grades nine and ten, in which students reflect on how authors transform source materials. At the end of high school, students in grades eleven and twelve devote their time to the works of eighteenth-, nineteenth-, and early-twentieth-century American literature with an emphasis on how multiple texts from the same time period treat similar themes or topics.

When reading informational texts, students in kindergarten through grade three dedicate their reading skills to the identification and comparison of multiple texts. In grade four, students use this integration of information in order to read or write about the topic themselves. Grade five marks the first year when students read more than two texts. This expectation builds in sixth, seventh, and eighth grades, when they begin to analyze these multiple approaches, culminating in grades nine through twelve with an evaluation of seminal fiction and nonfiction works.

Puppet Adventures

Comparing and contrasting texts requires a level of analysis that may be difficult for children in the early grades. For students who struggle with this skill, we find two strategies helpful. First, we chunk the process so they only have to do one specific task at a time. Second, we incorporate manipulatives so students have a built-in prompt that provides cues. Creating simple puppets for individual stories is a great way to integrate both strategies, and students love it!

Materials

- Several texts that feature a character who goes on an adventure
- Paper lunch bags
- Drawing materials

Directions

Read the text with students. Afterward, give each student a paper lunch bag to create a puppet. On one side, they will draw the character from the story. One the other, they will draw the story's setting. Encourage students to share their puppets, describing the characters, explaining the setting, and then using their puppets to retell what happened in the story. Read similar texts and follow this process for creating more puppets. Then ask each student to bring one puppet to the group and share his or her story. Be sure to structure the discussion toward the similarities and differences among the puppet adventures that students share.

Focus Questions

1. Who is the character in the story? How would you describe the character?
2. What is the setting of the story? When does the story happen? Where does the story happen?
3. What happens in the story? What happens first? Next? Then? How does the story end?
4. How are the adventures of the characters the same? How are they different?

Story Drop

Cueing systems are a powerful strategy to help struggling readers. A cue that students create is the ultimate—what better way to help them remember connections than from looking at their own work? We love "Story Drop" because it encourages students to use their own drawings to support learning.

Materials

- Two stories about a character who has an adventure
- Drawing materials: sheets of paper, crayons
- Tape or glue

Directions

Read the two stories with students. Then give them the drawing materials. Show students how to fold a sheet of paper in half. On one side of the paper, tell them to draw the character from the first story, and on the other side, draw the character from the second story. Talk about how the characters that students depict are similar to and different from one another. Next, give students a second sheet of paper and ask them to follow the same process to show the setting. After a discussion, give them a final sheet of paper. Encourage students to draw the characters' adventures in the same way. When students finish their drawings, glue or tape them together vertically to form drop panels as shown below. Using the drop panels, ask students to compare and contrast the two stories. If they struggle, remind them to look at their pictures.

Character 1	Character 2
Setting 1	Setting 2
Adventure 1	Adventure 2

Focus Questions

1. Who is the character in the story?
2. What is the story's setting?
3. What adventure does the character have?
4. How are the adventures the same? How are the adventures different?

● Double Take

As educators, we often focus on developing primary students' foundational literacy skills—to the neglect of developing their skills in text analysis. Working in tandem on these competencies, we begin by asking students to examine books visually. Removing written text from the equation frees students to investigate what they see, with no reading or listening required, just looking. Capitalizing on the confidence they gain from this task, we then scaffold them to investigate the written text. This sequence enables students to analyze more deeply and with the assurance of success.

Materials

- An informational book and a fictional story about the same subject (e.g., cats, families, the beach)

Directions

Read each text, and then place the books side by side. Ask students what differences they see between the two books. Focus on the visual elements first, drawing their attention to the photographs commonly found in nonfiction and illustrations more typical of fiction. Then move to the written text itself. What does the reader learn from the information book? The storybook? What similarities exist between the two books? What differences do they have?

Focus Questions

1. What kind of illustrations does this book have? What kind of illustrations does the other book have?

2. What did you learn in this book? What did you learn in the other book?

3. How are the books the same? How are they different?

4. Which book is your favorite? Why?

5. In which book did you learn the most? Why?

● Character Hat

Reading can be a very solitary practice—especially for struggling readers. We believe that it is not enough to teach skills. If we want to engage students and motivate them to read, we have to find ways that make reading fun and provide opportunities to encourage students to see reading as an activity they can enjoy with others. If you can do that, you are on your way to working with students who are excited to learn!

Materials

- A selection of books about a character who has an adventure (Also see pp. 119, 120.)
- Construction paper
- Scissors
- Tape
- Drawing supplies

Directions

Read the stories with students. Allow each student to pick a character from one of the stories. Help them make a character hat. The hat should reflect their character's personality and unique experiences. As students present their hats and discuss their characters, draw their attention to similarities and differences among the different adventures that the characters have.

Focus Questions

1. Who is the character in the story?

2. What adventure does the character go on?

3. How is the adventure the character has the same as the other characters' adventures? How is the adventure of the character different from the other characters' adventures?

Cinderella Scrapbook

Comparing and contrasting similar versions of the same narrative can be challenging—both in locating appropriate texts and in identifying a story that can maintain students' interest and engagement. Cinderella offers students not only a beloved story but also an opportunity to explore varied traditions and customs, as nearly every world culture has produced some version of the Cinderella story. While the theme remains the same, each version renders the narrative unique to its respective culture. The main character's name changes to reflect different languages, the setting moves to an appropriate location, the article that Cinderella loses (e.g., the shoe in the French version) also differs according to tradition, and the events follow the expectations for life in those cultures. For example, we all know the Disney version, but the Egyptian version sets the story during the time of the pharaohs, and the Cinderella archetype loses a sandal. One Mexican version takes place at a fiesta and suggests that the character loses her shawl. Nearly every culture has its own unique version of this story; narratives based on the Cinderella story number in the hundreds!

Materials

- Cinderella stories from multiple cultures (e.g., African, Caribbean, Chinese, Egyptian, French, German, Korean, Indian, Italian, Mexican, Native American, Russian, Vietnamese)
- Construction paper, white paper, and drawing materials for creating the scrapbook

Directions

Explain to students that they will be reading about how other countries have stories very similar to our Cinderella story and that they will begin a scrapbook about these different stories from around the world. The scrapbook should contain a page for each of the following components: (1) title of story and culture it is from, (2) name of Cinderella archetype with a drawing illustrating how she appears in the story, (3) a drawing of the setting that highlights how it is unique to this telling of the story, (4) a drawing of the article that the Cinderella character loses in the story, (5) a sequence of major events, and (6) what happens to the Cinderella character at the end of the story. As students continue reading the different Cinderella stories, emphasize how each version is both similar to the others and unique. Provide opportunities for students to share their scrapbooks with classmates.

Focus Questions

1. What is the name of the Cinderella character in this story? What does she look like? How is she similar to and different from the other Cinderella characters? Use details from the text to explain your answer.

2. Where is the story set? How is the setting similar to and different from the other stories? Use details from the text to explain your answer.

3. What item does this Cinderella character lose? How is it unique to this story? Use details from the text to explain your answer.

4. What happens in this Cinderella story? How is it similar to and different from the other stories? Use details from the text to explain your answer.

5. What happens to the Cinderella character at the end of the story? How is it similar to and different from the other stories? Use details from the text to explain your answer.

Action . . . Take Two!

Before comparing and contrasting narratives from different authors or cultures, we ask students to analyze a book in relation to a video. It provides skill building, but at a much less stressful level. After students experience success and feel confident, we move to comparing two texts. If students express anxiety, we just remind them that they have done it once already!

Materials

- A print and a video version of a popular folktale
- Chart paper and marker

Directions

Read the folktale with students. After thoroughly analyzing the text (e.g., character, setting, problem, solution, theme), show your students the video version of the story. Use the initial story analysis as a viewing guide, encouraging students to compare and contrast the video to the print version as they watch it. Afterward, lead a discussion about what students saw, and chart the similarities and differences.

Focus Questions

1. Who are the characters in this story? How would you describe them?
2. What is the setting? When does it happen? Where does it happen?
3. What is the problem in the story?
4. How is the problem solved in the story?
5. What lesson does the story teach?
6. How is the video similar to and different from the story?

One and the Same?

We often use a visual component in our lessons with struggling readers. It provides them with a structure to organize their thinking as well as a framework to record their learning. This visual component can be simple or elaborate . . . it only matters that you use it.

Materials

- A well-known folktale and a similar folktale with a different origin
- Chart paper and marker or interactive whiteboard

Directions

Read the first folktale with students, analyzing the characters, setting, problem, and solution. Then read the similar folktale and again plot the narrative elements of the story. Using a chart like the one below, discuss with students how the stories differ, why they differ, and which one they prefer.

	Story #1	Story #2
Characters		
Setting		
Problem		
Solution		

Focus Questions

1. Who are the characters in this story? How would you describe them? Why?
2. What is the setting in this story?
3. What is the problem in this story?
4. What is the solution in this story?
5. How are the narrative elements different in the other version of the story?
6. Why do you think the stories are different?
7. Does the overall story change? How? Why?
8. Which story do you like the most? Why?

Two Books and a Ball of Yarn!

Providing manipulatives should be a hallmark of working with struggling readers. We need to begin with the concrete before we move on to the abstract. This activity centers on developing students' awareness of similarities and differences among the main points that two texts make about a common subject. It's also a fun matching activity!

Materials

- Two informational texts about the same topic
- Sentence strips
- Markers or pencils
- Lengths of yarn (2 inches in length)
- Glue

Directions

Read the two texts with students. After completing the first book, ask students to identify its main points and help them write each main point on a separate sentence strip. Read the second book, and follow the same procedure. Next, lay the two sets of sentence strips side by side. After giving students lengths of yarn and glue, challenge them to find similarities between the texts' main points. When students locate a main point shared by both texts, have them connect the two points by gluing yarn to the two sentence strips. Explain to students that any sentence strips that are not connected with yarn shows where the two books differ.

Focus Questions

1. What are the main points in this book? How do you know?
2. What are the main points in the other book? How do you know?
3. Which points are the same?
4. Which points are different?

Author Studies

Author studies! What a wonderful source of reading for the struggling reader. The texts have familiar characters with recurring problems. The writing style is the same, and the texts are completely predictable. Author studies provide the perfect texts to teach comparing and contrasting. This activity also addresses CCSS in grades 2 and 3 that expect students to read stories from across the globe.

Materials

- A collection of texts by the same author
- A collection of texts with similar themes from multiple cultures

Directions

Provide students with multiple exposures to the stories of a particular author. Each time you read a story with students, highlight the theme. After students gain proficiency in identifying common themes, introduce texts from other cultures that share themes and discuss how different cultures treat the themes similarly and differently.

Focus Questions

1. What is theme?

2. What is the theme of this story? How do you know?

3. How do these two stories teach the same lesson? How are they similar? How are they different?

4. Why do you think the two stories are similar? Why are they different?

5. What can we learn about the way of life of the people in the story, based on the way the author chose to teach the lesson?

Author Studies Board Game

A game can make even the most arduous task fun. In the activity below, students play a simple board game to compare and contrast stories. We want students to develop their literacy skills, but it doesn't hurt to have a little fun along the way!

Materials and Preparation

- A collection of books by the same author
- Posterboard or cardboard
- Author Study Board Game (p. 129) for each group
- Glue or tape
- A die
- Game pieces, such as buttons, pasta, and so on

Attach a copy of the Author Study Board Game to a piece of posterboard or cardboard for each group.

Directions

After reading a number of texts by the same author, use the board game described below to review the texts. Instruct each student to play the game from the perspective of just one of the stories in the author's series.

Rules: Begin at Go. Throw the die. Move that number of spaces and answer the question. If you cannot answer the question correctly, you lose one turn. The first player to return to Go wins!

Focus Questions

Use the questions on the Author Study Board Game squares.

How is the solution in your story unlike other stories?	What is the theme of your story?	What is the setting of your story?	Jump two steps forward.
Return to GO.			How is the solution in your story like the other stories?
How is the problem in your story unlike the other stories?			How is the problem in your story like the other stories?
How is the theme in your story unlike the stories?	**Author Study Board Game**		Move back one step.
How is the setting in your story like the other stories?			How is your main character similar to those in other stories?
Who is the main character in your story?			How is the setting in your story unlike the other stories?
↑ GO	How is your main character unlike those in other stories?	Roll again.	How is the theme in your story like the other stories?

CHAPTER 10

A Variety of Genres and Text Complexity

Read and comprehend complex literary and informational texts independently and proficiently (CCSS, p. 10).

What students need to . . .

KNOW

- Literary texts
- Informational texts

UNDERSTAND

- Literature encompasses a broad range of literary genres (e.g., stories, drama, poetry) that offer unique perspectives to readers.
- Informational texts provide readers with knowledge.

DO

- Read complex literary and informational texts independently and proficiently.
- Comprehend complex literary and informational texts independently and proficiently.

Pedagogical Foundations

CCR10 emphasizes the absolute necessity of students developing reading skills at higher levels than are currently being reported by multiple national sources, including private-sector and federal and state studies. Although it is important for students to find a genre with which they have an affinity, it is equally critical that they experiment with and gain an appreciation of multiple genres (Calkins, 1994; Duke, Bennett-Armistead, & Roberts, 2002; Duke, Caughlan, Juzwik, & Martin, 2012; Duke & Roberts, 2010; Ranker, 2011; Smith, 1994). Similarly, allowing students to read at their independent reading level as a means of comfort and stability has real value to readers, especially struggling readers. Nonetheless, students must also be encouraged to push their skills to more advanced texts with appropriate scaffolding and interventions in place to ensure success (Brabham & Villaume, 2002; Coleman, 2011; Fisher, Frey, & Lapp, 2012; Gewertz, 2013; Hiebert & Pearson, 2010; Mesmer, Cunningham, & Hiebert, 2012; Shanahan, Fisher, & Frey, 2012). Taken together, this standard provides a significant foundation to move students forward in their overall reading experiences as well as in their development as learners and readers in a fast-developing technological world.

●●●●●●●●●●●

Transitional Steps for Student Mastery

In kindergarten, students begin with group reading activities. Grade-one students should be reading prose, poetry, and age-appropriate informational text. Grade-two students are expected to read at the high end of the grades 2–3 text-complexity range, and in grade three drama is added. Grade-four students are expected to read at the grades 4–5 text complexity band with scaffolding as needed. This scaffolding is taken away in grade five with students expected to read at the high end of the complexity band independently and proficiently. Students in grades six and seven should be reading at the high end of grades 6–8 complexity band with scaffolding as needed. They also begin reading literary nonfiction. Grade-eight students should read at the high end of this complexity independently and proficiently. Grade-nine students move to the high end of the grades 9–10 complexity band with scaffolding; grade-ten students read at the high end of the band independently and with proficiency. Grade-eleven students read in the high end of the grades 11–CCR text complexity band with scaffolding as needed. As with the previous grades, this scaffolding is removed in grade twelve with students expected to read independently and with proficiency at the high end of the range.

Text Complexity

The architects of Common Core State Standards fashioned CCR10 as the culmination of the previous nine standards. It builds on all of the other reading expectations and encompasses their skills in order to accomplish its goal of students reading across a wide range of genres and reading complexities. In effect, CCR10 collapses unless students experience rigorous instruction in CCR1–9. Of equal concern, however, remains the absolute necessity of exposing students to a diet of varied literary and informational text. To accomplish this, we need to address two questions: (1) What makes a text complex, and (2) how do we afford struggling students opportunities with these texts when they labor to make meaning from "easy" text? Because of the unique needs of Anchor Standard 10, the format of this chapter differs. Here, we analyze the true meaning of text complexity as well as offer scaffolding tips for greater range and text complexity.

Text complexity is a concept that many educators grapple with as they attempt to determine its influence in their instructional practice and as additional questions arise. What exactly does "complex" mean? How do we know if what students read rates as truly challenging? Can the same complex text be used for all our struggling students?

Let's begin with how we determine what makes a text complex. The Common Core State Standards Initiative suggests that these three factors constitute a rigorous text:

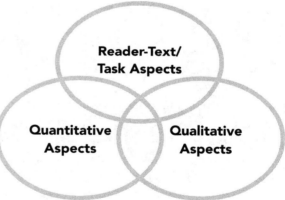

1. Quantitative aspects
2. Qualitative aspects
3. Matching the reader to both the text and the task assigned to it

Quantitative evaluation of texts refers to those aspects of the text that you can count and express in numbers.

- Look at the words in the text themselves. Are they one-syllable words, or are they multisyllabic? Longer words suggest a text will be more difficult for readers to comprehend.

- Consider word frequency. Are the words common in everyday reading, or are they rare—perhaps more academic or domain-specific?

- Move on to the sentences. Are they short, or are they long and syntactically complex?

- Now review the text as a whole. How long is it? Brief texts typically require less cognitive resources for students to make meaning. In the case of struggling readers, the longer the text, the harder it is for them to keep their grasp of individual words as they work to comprehend longer passages.

Targeted Reading Interventions for the Common Core © 2014 by Diana Sisson & Betsy Sisson, Scholastic Teaching Resources

Qualitative evaluation views the text through the lens of structure, language, and meaning.

- Can you identify the text structure? This is a significant aspect of the text; students who recognize the structure approach the reading differently because they are aware that the narrative or information will be presented in a unique way and are searching for signposts to guide their comprehension. Text structure also influences complexity, as it inherently alters the rigor of the content. For example, sequential passages follow a direct, easily observable flow of events or ideas—one after the other. Cause and effect, on the other hand, requires readers to differentiate between outcomes and causation with content that does not follow a linear progression, forcing students to classify content from throughout the text rather than in a chronological manner. In nonfiction text, specifically, text features expand the reading experience as they build a support system for accessing the content, but they require students to be familiar with them and how they function.

- Look at the text in a more global sense. Is the genre presenting the content in a simple or a sophisticated way? Does it demand domain-specific understanding?

- Examine the writing style of the author. Is it reader-friendly, or does it contain more sophisticated syntax?

- Look at the way the author uses language. Do you see examples of nonliteral language that fundamentally requires deeper understanding of vocabulary and how words and phrases are used?

- Survey the ideas and themes. Does the author describe them explicitly, or must readers draw conclusions and construct meaning independently?

The third factor shifts attention from the text to readers, centering on engagement. Think about these questions:

- Does the student have the background knowledge needed to access this text?
- Would this text interest or motivate the student to read?

Taken together, these factors present a framework to evaluate text complexity and determine how rigorous your expectations may be, taking into account the text and student. The next question is much more problematic: *How do we help struggling students access these texts with confidence and independence?*

Use the Text Complexity Checklist on the following page to determine the complexity of your texts and then make a decision as to their suitability for your students. Consider these questions: *Is the text too simple? Is it difficult? If so, will it become comprehensible to students with added support? Is the text so complex that students simply lack the resources to comprehend it?*

While the checklist will facilitate the selection of appropriate texts for your students, it's essential to expose them to a range of texts with varying levels of complexity. Thus, the last portion of this chapter offers 30 simple scaffolding tips to address Anchor Standard 10 and ensure that your students are on their way to becoming strong, independent readers and thinkers.

Text Complexity Checklist

Use this checklist to determine text complexity. Each item you check indicates an increase in the rigor of the text.

QUANTITATIVE EVALUATION

- [ ] Multisyllabic words
- [ ] Rarely used words; words from the academic domain
- [ ] Lengthy sentences
- [ ] Lengthy text
- [ ] Nonlinear text structure

QUALITATIVE EVALUATION

- [ ] Presence of text features (e.g., diagrams, graphs, charts, icons, sidebars, and so on)
- [ ] Sophisticated genre
- [ ] Unusual writing style
- [ ] Complex sentences
- [ ] Nonliteral language
- [ ] Implicit ideas or themes

READER AND TASK EVALUATION

- [ ] Prior knowledge needed
- [ ] Student interest lacking
- [ ] Student motivation lacking

30 Scaffolding Tips to Promote Greater Range and Text Complexity

Challenging text is often an insurmountable hurdle for educators. How do you help students who struggle to access on-level text approach readings that may be challenging for students who don't struggle? We recommend a variety of instructional support techniques. Each of them affords students a different means to learn as readers as well as to experience text in unique ways . . . and they reflect our instructional drivers for student success!

1. **Read-alouds** from text above students' independent reading level provide opportunities for students to engage with challenging ideas and literary themes without the difficulty of having to make sense of it on their own.

2. **Choral reading** offers students the ability to read in synchronization with their classmates, producing a safe setting where they can read and learn collaboratively.

3. **High-frequency word study** develops vocabulary skills that free up cognitive resources at the word level so students can read for meaning.

4. **Repeated readings** present multiple exposures with text so students have opportunities to comprehend at deeper levels.

5. **Songs** supply text in an engaging format that supports student comprehension and motivation.

6. **Poems** encourage wordplay and render short pieces of text in manageable chunks.

7. **Informational texts** appear less regularly than fictional selections so students are less comfortable with those texts. Informational texts also require reading skills and strategies unique to their genre, which will necessitate explicit instruction.

8. **Paired reading** furnishes students with a partner with whom to read and grapple with meaning in a cooperative, safe environment.

9. **Echo reading** is an instructional scaffold that allows students to hear demanding text read aloud as a model before they attempt to read it independently.

10. **Guided oral retelling** chunks student comprehension into meaningful parts with ongoing instructional support.

11. **Think-alouds** reveal how good readers approach text and the strategies they employ when meaning breaks down.

12. **Books on tape** grant struggling readers the benefits of the content of rigorous text while eliminating the reluctance to read normally associated with challenging writing.

13. **Predictable stories** increase students' understanding of story grammar, thereby developing their skills for more sophisticated narratives.

14. **Varied genres** included in the reading program foster students' appreciation of text in multiple styles and purposes.

15. **Predictions** before, during, and after reading engage students in the reading process and enable you to monitor their comprehension.

16. **Illustrations** underpin text content and can reinforce student comprehension.

17. **Story grammar (character, setting, problem, solution)** provides a framework for struggling students to focus their attention on when reading narratives.

18. **Author/illustrator studies** provide stability and comfort for students who find the reading experience murky and perplexing.

19. **Visualization** bridges the gap between the abstract nature of text and the concrete images that words create. It offers struggling readers an anchor to hold onto as they endeavor to make meaningful connections.

20. **Silent sustained reading** promises the one thing that all struggling readers need—time to practice.

21. **Fluency activities** increase students' accuracy and automaticity when reading, which transfers their mental processes from the word level to making meaning.

22. **Readers Theater** hands students a short, engaging text read collaboratively, which provides multiple supports.

23. **Genre characteristic knowledge** acts much like predictable text or story grammar in that it arms struggling students with a valuable tool for the reading process.

24. **Literature circles** supply a built-in support system by allowing struggling students to encounter text in a collaborative environment, read and complete activities with classmates, and have ongoing teacher interaction.

25. **Concept mapping** enables students to build understanding of content knowledge using a supportive, visual technique.

26. **Figurative language study** equips students with an understanding of the kind of nonliteral language prevalent in texts throughout grades and across academic domains.

27. **Think-pair-share** matches students with a partner with whom they can confer as they attempt to process text and comprehend its intent and meaning.

28. **Graphic aids** support comprehension and provide suggestions to struggling students on how to approach the reading process.

29. **Kinesthetic activities** employ multiple modalities of learning and motivate students in ways that other strategies cannot.

30. **Probing for inferential thinking** bridges the gap between the literal level of comprehension and the acquisition of critical analysis skills that students need to become independent readers.

Targeted Reading Interventions for the Common Core © 2014 by Diana Sisson & Betsy Sisson, Scholastic Teaching Resources

Appendix A

COMMON CORE STATE STANDARDS FOR ENGLISH LANGUAGE ARTS & LITERACY IN HISTORY/SOCIAL STUDIES, SCIENCE, AND TECHNICAL SUBJECTS: AN OVERVIEW

What are the Common Core State Standards (CCSS)?

- Coordinated by the National Governors Association (NGA) and the Council of Chief State School Officers (CCSSO)
- Benchmarked with international standards
- Correlated with college and career expectations
- Aligned with NAEP Reading Framework
- Encompassing broad expectations that are cumulative and scaffolded for K–12 for both literary and nonfiction texts
- Sets grade-level expectations

What are the limitations of the Common Core State Standards?

- No prescription for how to teach
- No description of accelerated study
- No explanation of intervention supports
- No specialized plan for ELL or special needs students

What is the design of the CCSS?

- K–5 (cross-disciplinary)
- 6–12 English Language Arts
- 6–12 Literacy in History/Social Studies, Science, and Technical Subjects

COLLEGE AND CAREER READINESS
ANCHOR STANDARDS FOR READING

Key Ideas and Details

1. Read closely to determine what the text says explicitly and to make logical references from it; cite specific textual evidence when writing or speaking to support conclusions drawn from the text.

2. Determine central ideas or themes of a text and analyze their development; summarize the key supporting details and ideas.

3. Analyze how and why individuals, events, and ideas develop and interact over the course of a text.

Craft and Structure

4. Interpret words and phrases as they are used in a text, including determining technical, connotative, and figurative meanings, and analyze how specific word choices shape meaning or tone.

5. Analyze the structure of texts, including how specific sentences, paragraphs, and larger portions of the text (e.g., a section, chapter, scene, or stanza) relate to each other and the whole.

6. Assess how point of view or purpose shapes the content and style of a text.

Integration of Knowledge and Ideas

7. Integrate and evaluate content presented in diverse media and formats, including visually and quantitatively, as well as in words.

8. Delineate and evaluate the argument and specific claims in a text, including the validity of the reasoning as well as the relevance and sufficiency of the evidence.

9. Analyze how two or more texts address similar themes or topics in order to build knowledge or to compare the approaches the authors take.

Range of Reading and Level of Text Complexity

10. Read and comprehend complex literary and informational texts independently and proficiently.

Source: *http://www.corestandards.org/assets/CCSSI_ELA%20Standards.pdf*

STANDARDS FOR LITERATURE

STANDARD 1

Read closely to determine what the text says explicitly and to make logical inferences from it; cite specific textual evidence when writing or speaking to support conclusions drawn from the text.

Kindergarten	Grade 1	Grade 2
With prompting and support, ask and answer questions about key details in a text.	Ask and answer questions about key details in a text.	Ask and answer such questions as who, what, where, when, why, and how to demonstrate understanding of key details in a text.

Grade 3	Grade 4	Grade 5
Ask and answer questions to demonstrate understanding of a text, referring explicitly to the text as the basis for the answers.	Refer to details and examples in a text when explaining what the text says explicitly and when drawing inferences from the text.	Quote accurately from a text when explaining what the text says explicitly and when drawing inferences from the text.

Grade 6	Grade 7	Grade 8
Cite textual evidence to support analysis of what the text says explicitly as well as inferences drawn from the text.	Cite several pieces of textual evidence to support analysis of what the text says explicitly as well as inferences from the text.	Cite the textual evidence that most strongly supports an analysis of what the text says explicitly as well as inferences drawn from the text.

Grades 9–10	Grades 11–12
Cite strong and thorough textual evidence to support analysis of what the text says explicitly as well as inferences drawn from the text.	Cite strong and thorough textual evidence to support analysis of what the text says explicitly as well as inferences drawn from the text, including determining where the text leaves matters uncertain.

STANDARD 2

Determine central ideas or themes of a text and analyze their development; summarize the key supporting details and ideas.

Kindergarten	Grade 1	Grade 2
With prompting and support, retell familiar stories, including key details.	Retell stories, including key details, and demonstrate understanding of their central message or lesson.	Recount stories, including fables and folktales from diverse cultures, and determine their central message, lesson, or moral.

Grade 3	Grade 4	Grade 5
Recount stories, including fables, folktales, and myths from diverse cultures; determine the central message, lesson, or moral and explain how it is conveyed through key details in the text.	Determine the theme of a story, drama, or poem from details in the text; summarize the text.	Determine a theme of a story, drama, or poem from details in the text, including how characters in a story or drama respond to challenges or how the speaker in a poem reflects upon a topic; summarize the text.

Grade 6	Grade 7	Grade 8
Determine a theme or central idea of a text and how it is conveyed through particular details; provide a summary of the text distinct from personal opinions or judgments.	Determine a theme or central idea of a text and analyze its development over the course of the text; provide an objective summary of the text.	Determine a theme or central idea of a text and analyze its development over the course of the text, including its relationship to the characters, setting, and plot; provide an objective summary of the text.

Grades 9–10	Grades 11–12
Determine a theme or central idea of a text and analyze in detail its development over the course of the text, including how it emerges and is shaped and refined by specific details; provide an objective summary of the text.	Determine two or more themes or central ideas of a text and analyze their development over the course of the text, including how they interact and build on one another to produce a complex account; provide an objective summary of the text.

STANDARD 3

Analyze how and why individuals, events, and ideas develop and interact over the course of a text.

Kindergarten	Grade 1	Grade 2
With prompting and support, identify characters, settings, and major events in a story.	Describe characters, settings, and major events in a story, using key details.	Describe how characters in a story respond to major events and challenges.
Grade 3	**Grade 4**	**Grade 5**
Describe characters in a story (e.g., their traits, motivations, or feelings) and explain how their actions contribute to the sequence of events.	Describe in depth a character, setting, or event in a story or drama, drawing on specific details in the text (e.g., a character's thoughts, words or actions).	Compare and contrast two or more characters, settings, or events in a story or drama, drawing on specific details in the text (e.g., how characters interact).
Grade 6	**Grade 7**	**Grade 8**
Describe how a particular story's or drama's plot unfolds in a series of episodes as well as how the characters respond or change as the plot moves toward a resolution.	Analyze how particular elements of a story or drama interact (e.g., how setting shapes the characters or plot).	Analyze how particular lines of dialogue or incidents in a story or drama propel the action, reveal aspects of a character, or provoke a decision.

Grades 9–10	Grades 11–12
Analyze how complex characters (e.g., those with multiple or conflicting motivations) develop over the course of a text, interact with other characters, and advance the plot or develop the theme.	Analyze the impact of the author's choices regarding how to develop and relate elements of a story or drama (e.g., where a story is set, how the action is ordered, how the characters are introduced and developed).

STANDARD 4

Interpret words and phrases as they are used in a text, including determining technical, connotative, and figurative meanings, and analyze how specific word choices shape meaning or tone.

Kindergarten	Grade 1	Grade 2
Ask and answer questions about unknown words in a text.	Identify words and phrases in stories or poems that suggest feelings or appeal to the senses.	Describe how words and phrases (e.g., regular beats, alliteration, rhymes, repeated lines) supply rhythm and meaning in a story, poem, or song.
Grade 3	**Grade 4**	**Grade 5**
Determine the meaning of words and phrases as they are used in a text, distinguishing literal from nonliteral language.	Determine the meaning of words and phrases as they are used in a text, including those that allude to significant characters found in mythology (e.g., Herculean).	Determine the meaning of words and phrases as they are used in a text, including figurative language such as metaphors and similes.

Targeted Reading Interventions for the Common Core © 2014 by Diana Sisson & Betsy Sisson, Scholastic Teaching Resources

Grade 6	Grade 7	Grade 8
Determine the meaning of words and phrases as they are used in a text, including figurative and connotative meanings; analyze the impact of a specific word choice on meaning and tone.	Determine the meaning of words and phrases as they are used in a text, including figurative and connotative meanings; analyze the impact of rhymes and other repetitions of sounds (e.g., alliteration) on a specific verse or stanza of a poem or section of a story or drama.	Determine the meaning of words and phrases as they are used in a text, including figurative and connotative meanings; analyze the impact of specific word choices on meaning and tone, including analogies or allusions to other texts.

Grades 9–10	Grades 11–12
Determine the meaning of words and phrases as they are used in the text, including figurative and connotative meanings; analyze the cumulative impact of specific word choices on meaning and tone (e.g., how the language evokes a sense of time and place; how it sets a formal or informal tone).	Determine the meaning of words and phrases as they are used in the text, including figurative and connotative meanings; analyze the impact of specific word choices on meaning and tone, including words with multiple meanings or language that is particularly fresh, engaging, or beautiful. (Include Shakespeare as well as other authors).

STANDARD 5

Analyze the structure of texts, including how specific sentences, paragraphs, and larger portions of the text (e.g., a section, chapter, scene, or stanza) relate to each other and the whole.

Kindergarten	Grade 1	Grade 2
Recognize common types of texts (e.g., storybooks, poems).	Explain major differences between books that tell stories and books that give information, drawing on a wide range or text types.	Describe the overall structure of a story, including describing how the beginning introduces the story and the ending concludes the action.

Grade 3	Grade 4	Grade 5
Refer to parts of stories, dramas, and poems when writing or speak about a text, using terms such as chapter, scene, and stanza; describe how each successive part builds on earlier sections.	Explain major differences between poems, drama, and prose, and refer to the structural elements of poems (e.g., verse, rhythm, meter) and drama (e.g., casts of characters, settings, descriptions, dialogue, stage directions) when writing or speaking about a text.	Explain how a series of chapters, scenes, or stanzas fit together to provide the overall structure of a particular story, drama, or poem.

Grade 6	Grade 7	Grade 8
Analyze how a particular sentence, chapter, scene, or stanza fits into the overall structure of a text and contributes to the development of theme, setting, or plot.	Analyze how a drama's or poem's form or structure (e.g., soliloquy, sonnet) contributes to its meaning.	Compare and contrast the structure of two or more texts and analyze how the differing structure of each text contributes to its meaning and style.

Grades 9–10	Grades 11–12
Analyze how an author's choices concerning how to structure a text, order events within it (e.g., parallel plots) and manipulate time (e.g., pacing, flashbacks) create such effects as mystery, tension, or surprise.	Analyze how an author's choices concerning how to structure specific parts of a text (e.g., the choice of where to begin or end a story, the choice to provide a comedic or tragic resolution) contribute to its overall structure and meaning as well as its aesthetic impact.

STANDARD 6

Assess how point of view or purpose shapes the content and style of a text.

Kindergarten	Grade 1	Grade 2
With prompting and support, name the author and illustrator of a story and define the role of each in telling the story.	Identify who is telling the story at various points in a text.	Acknowledge differences in the points of view of characters, including by speaking in a different voice for each character when reading dialogue aloud.

Grade 3	Grade 4	Grade 5
Distinguish their own point of view from that of the narrator or those of the characters.	Compare and contrast the point of view from which different stories are narrated, including the difference between first- and third-person narrations.	Describe how a narrator's or speaker's point of view influences how events are described.

Grade 6	Grade 7	Grade 8
Explain how an author develops the point of view of the narrator or speaker in a text.	Analyze how an author develops and contrasts the points of view of different characters or narrators in a text.	Analyze how differences in the points of view of the characters and the audience or reader (e.g., created through the use of dramatic irony) create such effects as suspense or humor.

Grades 9–10		Grades 11–12	
Analyze a particular point of view or cultural experience reflected in a work of literature from outside the United States, drawing on a wide reading of world literature.		Analyze a case in which grasping point of view requires distinguishing what is directly stated in a text from what is really meant (e.g., satire, sarcasm, irony, or understatement).	

STANDARD 7

Integrate and evaluate content presented in diverse media and formats, including visually and quantitatively, as well as in words.

Kindergarten	Grade 1	Grade 2
With prompting and support, describe the relationship between illustrations and the story in which they appear (e.g., what moment in a story an illustration depicts).	Use illustrations and details in a story to describe its characters, setting, or events.	Use information gained from the illustrations and words in a print or digital text to demonstrate understanding of its characters, setting, or plot.

Grade 3	Grade 4	Grade 5
Explain how specific aspects of a text's illustrations contribute to what is conveyed by the words in a story (e.g., create mood, emphasize aspects of a character or setting).	Make connections between the text of a story or drama and a visual or oral presentation of the text, identifying where each version reflects specific descriptions and directions in the text.	Analyze how visual and multimedia elements contribute to the meaning, tone, or beauty of a text (e.g., graphic novel, multimedia presentation of fiction, folktale, myth, poem).

Grade 6	Grade 7	Grade 8
Compare and contrast the experience of reading a story, drama, or poem to listening to or viewing an audio, video, or live version of the text, including contrasting what they "see" and "hear" when reading the text to what they perceive when they listen or watch.	Compare and contrast a written story, drama, or poem to its audio, filmed, staged, or multimedia version, analyzing the effects of techniques unique to each medium (e.g., lighting, sound, color, or camera focus and angles in a film).	Analyze the extent to which a filmed or live production of a story or drama stays faithful to or departs from the text or script, evaluating the choices made by the director or actors.

Grades 9–10	Grades 11–12
Analyze the representation of a subject or a key scene in two different artistic mediums, including what is emphasized or absent in each treatment (e.g., Auden's "Musée des Beaux Arts" and Breughel's *Landscape with the Fall of Icarus*).	Analyze multiple interpretations of a story, drama, or poem (e.g., recorded or live production of a play or recorded novel or poetry), evaluating how each version interprets the source text. (Include at least one play by Shakespeare and one play by an American dramatist.)

STANDARD 8

Delineate and evaluate the argument and specific claims in a text, including the validity of the reasoning as well as the relevance and sufficiency of the evidence.

Not applicable to literature

STANDARD 9

Analyze how two or more texts address similar themes or topics in order to build knowledge or to compare the approaches the authors take.

Kindergarten	Grade 1	Grade 2
With prompting and support, compare and contrast the adventures and experiences of characters in familiar stories.	Compare and contrast the adventures and experiences of characters in stories.	Compare and contrast two or more versions of the same story (e.g., Cinderella stories) by different authors or from different cultures.

Grade 3	Grade 4	Grade 5
Compare and contrast the themes, settings, and plots of stories written by the same author about the same or similar characters (e.g., in books from a series).	Compare and contrast the treatment of similar themes and topics (e.g., opposition of good and evil) and patterns of events (e.g., the quest) in stories, myths, and traditional literature from different cultures.	Compare and contrast stories in the same genre (e.g., mysteries and adventure stories) on their approaches to similar themes and topics.

Grade 6	Grade 7	Grade 8
Compare and contrast texts in different forms or genres (e.g., stories and poems, historical novels and fantasy stories) in terms of their approaches to similar themes and topics.	Compare and contrast a fictional portrayal of a time, place, or character, and a historical account of the same period as a means of understanding how authors of fiction use or alter history.	Analyze how a modern work of fiction draws on themes, patterns of events, or character types from myths, traditional stories, or religious works such as the Bible, including describing how the material is rendered new.

Grades 9–10	Grades 11–12
Analyze how an author draws on and transforms source materials in a specific work (e.g., how Shakespeare treats a theme or topic from Ovid or the Bible or how a later author draws on a play by Shakespeare).	Demonstrate knowledge of eighteenth-, nineteenth-, and early-twentieth-century foundational works of American literature, including how two or more texts from the same period treat similar themes or topics.

STANDARD 10

Read and comprehend complex literary and informational texts independently and proficiently.

Kindergarten	Grade 1	Grade 2
Actively engage in group reading activities with purpose and understanding.	With prompting and support, read prose and poetry of appropriate complexity for grade 1.	By the end of the year, read and comprehend literature, including stories and poetry, in the grades 2–3 complexity band proficiently, with scaffolding as needed at the high end of the range.

Grade 3	Grade 4	Grade 5
By the end of the year, read and comprehend literature, including stories, dramas, and poetry at the high end of the grades 2–3 complexity band independently and proficiently.	By the end of the year, read and comprehend literature, including stories, dramas, and poetry, in the grades 4–5 complexity band proficiently, with scaffolding as needed at the high end of the range.	By the end of the year, read and comprehend literature, including stories, drama, and poetry, at the high end of the grades 4–5 complexity band independently and proficiently.

Grade 6	Grade 7	Grade 8
By the end of the year, read and comprehend literature, including stories, dramas, and poems, in the grades 6–8 complexity band proficiently, with scaffolding as needed at the high end of the range.	By the end of the year, read and comprehend literature, including stories, dramas, and poems, in the grades 6–8 complexity band proficiently, with scaffolding as needed at the high end of the range.	By the end of the year, read and comprehend literature, including stories, dramas, and poems, at the high end of the grades 6–8 complexity bank independently and proficiently.

Grades 9–10		Grades 11–12
By the end of grade 9, read and comprehend literature, including stories, dramas, and poems, in the grades 9–10 text complexity band proficiently, with scaffolding as needed at the high end of the range. By the end of grade 10, read and comprehend literature, including stories, dramas, and poems, at the high end of the grades 9–10 text complexity band independently and proficiently.		By the end of grade 11, read and comprehend literature, including stories, dramas, or poems, in the grades 11-CCR text complexity band proficiently, with scaffolding as needed at the high end of the range. By the end of grade 12, read and comprehend literature, including stories, dramas, and poems, at the high end of the grades 11-CCR text complexity band independently and proficiently.

Source: *http://www.corestandards.org/assets/CCSSI_ELA%20Standards.pdf*

STANDARDS FOR INFORMATIONAL TEXT

STANDARD 1

Read closely to determine what the text says explicitly and to make logical inferences from it; cite specific textual evidence when writing or speaking to support conclusions drawn from the text.

Kindergarten	Grade 1	Grade 2
With prompting and support, ask and answer questions about key details in a text.	Ask and answer questions about key details in a text.	Ask and answer such questions as who, what, where, when, why, and how to demonstrate understanding of key details in a text.

Grade 3	Grade 4	Grade 5
Ask and answer questions to demonstrate understanding of a text, referring explicitly to the text as the basis for the answers.	Refer to details and examples in a text when explaining what the text says explicitly and when drawing inferences from the text.	Quote accurately from a text when explaining what the text says explicitly and when drawing inferences from the text.

Grade 6	Grade 7	Grade 8
Cite textual evidence to support analysis of what the text says explicitly as well as inferences drawn from the text.	Cite several pieces of textual evidence to support analysis of what the text says explicitly as well as inferences drawn from the text.	Cite the textual evidence that most strongly supports an analysis of what the text says explicitly as well as inferences drawn from the text.

Grades 9–10	Grades 11–12
Cite strong and thorough textual evidence to support analysis of what the text says explicitly as well as inferences drawn from the text.	Cite strong and thorough textual evidence to support analysis of what the text says explicitly as well as inferences drawn from the text, including determining where the text leaves matters uncertain.

STANDARD 2

Determine central ideas or themes of a text and analyze their development; summarize the key supporting details and ideas.

Kindergarten	Grade 1	Grade 2
With prompting and support, identify the main topic and retell key details of a text.	Identify the main topic and retell key details of a text.	Identify the main topic of a multiparagraph text as well as the focus of specific paragraphs within the text.

Grade 3	Grade 4	Grade 5
Determine the main idea of a text; recount the key details and explain how they support the main idea.	Determine the main idea of a text and explain how it is supported by key details; summarize the text.	Determine two or more main ideas of a text and explain how they are supported by key details; summarize the text.

Grade 6	Grade 7	Grade 8
Determine a central idea of a text and how it is conveyed through particular details; provide a summary of the text distinct from personal opinions or judgments.	Determine two or more central ideas in a text and analyze their development over the course of the text; provide an objective summary of the text.	Determine a central idea of a text and analyze its development over the course of the text, including its relationship to supporting ideas; provide an objective summary of the text.

Grades 9–10	Grades 11–12
Determine a central idea of a text and analyze its development over the course of the text, including how it emerges and is shaped and refined by specific details; provide an objective summary of the text.	Determine two or more central ideas of a text and analyze their development over the course of the text, including how they interact and build on one another to provide a complex analysis; provide an objective summary of the text.

STANDARD 3

Analyze how and why individuals, events, and ideas develop and interact over the course of a text.

Kindergarten	Grade 1	Grade 2
With prompting and support, describe the connection between two individuals, events, ideas, or pieces of information in a text.	Describe the connection between two individuals, events, ideas, or pieces of information in a text.	Describe the connection between a series of historical events, scientific ideas or concepts, or steps in technical procedures in a text.
Grade 3	**Grade 4**	**Grade 5**
Describe the relationship between a series of historical events, scientific ideas or concepts, or steps in technical procedures in a text, using language that pertains to time, sequence, and cause/effect.	Explain events, procedures, ideas, or concepts in a historical, scientific, or technical text, including what happened and why, based on specific information in the text.	Explain the relationships or interactions between two or more individuals, events, ideas, or concepts in a historical, scientific, or technical text based on specific information in the text.
Grade 6	**Grade 7**	**Grade 8**
Analyze in detail how a key individual, event, or idea is introduced, illustrated, and elaborated in a text (e.g., through examples or anecdotes).	Analyze the interactions between individuals, events, and ideas in a text (e.g., how ideas influence individuals or events, or how individuals influence ideas or events).	Analyze how a text makes connections among and distinctions between individuals, ideas, or events (e.g., through comparisons, analogies, or categories).

Grades 9–10	Grades 11–12
Analyze how the author unfolds an analysis or series of ideas or events, including the order in which the points are made, how they are introduced and developed, and the connections that are drawn between them.	Analyze a complex set of ideas or sequence of events and explain how specific individuals, ideas, or events interact and develop over the course of the text.

STANDARD 4

Interpret words and phrases as they are used in a text, including determining technical, connotative, and figurative meanings, and analyze how specific word choices shape meaning or tone.

Kindergarten	Grade 1	Grade 2
With prompting and support, ask and answer questions about unknown words in a text.	Ask and answer questions to help determine or clarify the meaning of words and phrases in a text.	Determine the meaning of words and phrases in a text relevant to a grade 2 topic or subject area.
Grade 3	**Grade 4**	**Grade 5**
Determine the meaning of general academic and domain-specific words and phrases in a text relevant to a grade 3 topic or subject area.	Determine the meaning of general academic and domain-specific words or phrases in a text relevant to a grade 4 topic or subject area.	Determine the meaning of general academic and domain-specific words and phrases in a text relevant to a grade 5 topic or subject area.

Grade 6	Grade 7	Grade 8
Determine the meaning of words and phrases as they are used in a text, including figurative, connotative, and technical meanings.	Determine the meaning of words and phrases as they are used in a text, including figurative, connotative, and technical meanings; analyze the impact of a specific word choice on meaning and tone.	Determine the meaning of words and phrases as they are used in a text, including figurative, connotative, and technical meanings; analyze the impact of specific word choices on meaning and tone, including analogies or allusions to other texts.

Grades 9–10	Grades 11–12
Determine the meaning of words and phrases as they are used in a text, including figurative, connotative, and technical meanings; analyze the cumulative impact of specific word choices on meaning and tone (e.g., how the language of a court opinion differs from that of a newspaper).	Determine the meaning of words and phrases as they are used in a text, including figurative, connotative, and technical meanings; analyze how an author uses and refines the meaning of a key term or terms over the course of a text (e.g., how Madison defines *faction* in *Federalist* No. 10).

STANDARD 5

Analyze the structure of texts, including how specific sentences, paragraphs, and larger portions of the text (e.g., a section, chapter, scene, or stanza) relate to each other and the whole.

Kindergarten	Grade 1	Grade 2
Identify the front cover, back cover, and title page of a book.	Know and use various text features (e.g., headings, tables of contents, glossaries, electronic menus, icons) to locate key facts or information in a text.	Know and use various text features (e.g., captions, bold print, subheadings, glossaries, indexes, electronic menus, icons) to locate key facts or information in a text efficiently.

Grade 3	Grade 4	Grade 5
Use text features and search tools (e.g., key words, sidebars, hyperlinks) to locate information relevant to a given topic efficiently.	Describe the overall structure (e.g., chronology, comparison, cause/effect, problem/solution) of events, ideas, concepts, or information in a text or part of a text.	Compare and contrast the overall structure (e.g., chronology, comparison, cause/effect, problem/solution) of events, ideas, concepts, or information in two or more texts.

Grade 6	Grade 7	Grade 8
Analyze how a particular sentence, paragraph, chapter, or section fits into the overall structure of a text and contributes to the development of the ideas.	Analyze the structure an author uses to organize a text, including how the major sections contribute to the whole and to the development of the ideas.	Analyze in detail the structure of a specific paragraph in a text, including the role of particular sentences in developing and refining a key concept.

Grades 9–10	Grades 11–12
Analyze in detail how an author's ideas or claims are developed and refined by particular sentences, paragraphs, or larger portions of a text (e.g., a section or chapter).	Analyze and evaluate the effectiveness of the structure an author uses in his or her exposition or argument, including whether the structure makes points clear, convincing, and engaging.

STANDARD 6

Assess how point of view or purpose shapes the content and style of a text.

Kindergarten	Grade 1	Grade 2
Name the author and illustrator of a text and define the role of each in presenting the ideas or information in a text.	Distinguish between information provided by pictures or other illustrations and information provided by the words in a text.	Identify the main purpose of a text, including what the author wants to answer, explain, or describe.

Grade 3	Grade 4	Grade 5
Distinguish their own point of view from that of the author of a text.	Compare and contrast a firsthand and secondhand account of the same event or topic; describe the differences in focus and the information provided.	Analyze multiple accounts of the same event or topic, noting important similarities and differences in the point of view they represent.

Grade 6	Grade 7	Grade 8
Determine an author's point of view or purpose in a text and explain how it is conveyed in the text.	Determine an author's point of view or purpose in a text and analyze how the author distinguishes his or her position from that of others.	Determine an author's point of view or purpose in a text and analyze how the author acknowledges and responds to conflicting evidence or viewpoints.

Grades 9–10	Grades 11–12
Determine an author's point of view or purpose in a text and analyze how an author uses rhetoric to advance that point of view or purpose.	Determine an author's point of view or purpose in a text in which the rhetoric is particularly effective, analyzing how style and content contribute to the power, persuasiveness or beauty of the text.

STANDARD 7

Assess how point of view or purpose shapes the content and style of a text.

Kindergarten	Grade 1	Grade 2
With prompting and support, describe the relationship between illustrations and the text in which they appear (e.g., what person, place, thing, or idea in the text an illustration depicts).	Use the illustrations and details in a text to describe its key ideas.	Explain how specific images (e.g., a diagram showing how a machine works) contribute to and clarify a text.

Grade 3	Grade 4	Grade 5
Use information gained from illustrations (e.g., maps, photographs) and the words in a text to demonstrate understanding of the text (e.g., where, when, why, and how key events occur).	Interpret information presented visually, orally, or quantitatively (e.g., in charts, graphs, diagrams, time lines, animations, or interactive elements on Web pages) and explain how the information contributes to an understanding of the text in which it appears.	Draw on information from multiple print or digital sources, demonstrating the ability to locate an answer to a question quickly or to solve a problem efficiently.

Grade 6	Grade 7	Grade 8
Integrate information presented in different media or formats (e.g., visually, quantitatively) as well as in words to develop a coherent understanding of a topic or issue.	Compare and contrast a text to an audio, video, or multimedia version of the text, analyzing each medium's portrayal of the subject (e.g., how the delivery of a speech affects the impact of the words).	Evaluate the advantages and disadvantages of using different mediums (e.g., print or digital text, video, multimedia) to present a particular topic or idea.

Grades 9–10	Grades 11–12
Analyze various accounts of a subject told in different mediums (e.g., a person's life story in both print and multimedia), determining which details are emphasized in each account.	Integrate and evaluate multiple sources of information presented in different media or formats (e.g., visually, quantitatively) as well as in words in order to address a question or solve a problem.

STANDARD 8

Delineate and evaluate the argument and specific claims in a text, including the validity of the reasoning as well as the relevance and sufficiency of the evidence.

Kindergarten	Grade 1	Grade 2
With prompting and support, identify the reasons an author gives to support points in a text.	Identify the reasons an author gives to support points in a text.	Describe how reasons support specific points the author makes in a text.

Grade 3	Grade 4	Grade 5
Describe the logical connection between particular sentences and paragraphs in a text (e.g., comparison, cause/effect, first/second/third in a sequence).	Explain how an author uses reasons and evidence to support particular points in a text.	Explain how an author uses reasons and evidence to support particular points in a text, identifying which reasons and evidence support which point(s).

Grade 6	Grade 7	Grade 8
Trace and evaluate the argument and specific claims in a text, distinguishing claims that are supported by reasons and evidence from claims that are not.	Trace and evaluate the argument and specific claims in a text, assessing whether the reasoning is sound and the evidence is relevant and sufficient to support the claims.	Delineate and evaluate the argument and specific claims in a text, assessing whether the reasoning is sound and the evidence is relevant and sufficient; recognize when irrelevant evidence is introduced.

Grades 9–10		Grades 11–12
Delineate and evaluate the argument and specific claims in a text, assessing whether the reasoning is valid and the evidence is relevant and sufficient; identify false statements and fallacious reasoning.		Delineate and evaluate the reasoning in seminal U.S. texts, including the application of constitutional principles and use of legal reasoning (e.g., in U.S. Supreme Court majority opinions and dissents) and the premises, purposes, and arguments in works of public advocacy (e.g., *The Federalist*, presidential addresses).

STANDARD 9

Analyze how two or more texts address similar themes or topics in order to build knowledge or to compare the approaches the authors take.

Kindergarten	Grade 1	Grade 2
With prompting and support, identify basic similarities in and differences between two texts on the same topic (e.g., in illustrations, descriptions, or procedures).	Identify basic similarities in and differences between two texts on the same topic (e.g., in illustrations, descriptions, or procedures).	Compare and contrast the most important points presented by two texts on the same topic.

Grade 3	Grade 4	Grade 5
Compare and contrast the most important points and key details presented in two texts on the same topic.	Integrate information from two texts on the same topic in order to write or speak about the subject knowledgeably.	Integrate information from several texts on the same topic in order to write or speak about the subject knowledgeably.

Grade 6	Grade 7	Grade 8
Compare and contrast one author's presentation of events with that of another (e.g., a memoir written by and a biography on the same person).	Analyze how two or more authors writing about the same topic shape their presentations of key information by emphasizing different evidence or advancing different interpretations of facts.	Analyze a case in which two or more texts provide conflicting information on the same topic and identify where the texts disagree on matters of fact or interpretation.

Grades 9–10	Grades 11–12
Analyze seminal U.S. documents of historical and literary significance (e.g., Washington's Farewell Address, the Gettysburg Address, Roosevelt's Four Freedoms speech, King's "Letter from Birmingham Jail"), including how they address related themes and concepts.	Analyze seventeenth-, eighteenth-, and nineteenth-century foundational U.S. documents of historical and literary significance (including The Declaration of Independence, the Preamble to the Constitution, the Bill of Rights, and Lincoln's Second Inaugural Address) for their themes, purposes, and rhetorical features.

STANDARD 10

Read and comprehend complex literary and informational texts independently and proficiently.

Kindergarten	Grade 1	Grade 2
Actively engage in group reading activities with purpose and understanding.	With prompting and support, read informational texts appropriately complex for grade 1.	By the end of year, read and comprehend informational texts, including history/social studies, science, and technical texts, in the grades 2–3 text complexity band proficiently, with scaffolding as needed at the high end of the range.

Grade 3	Grade 4	Grade 5
By the end of the year, read and comprehend informational texts, including history/social studies, science, and technical texts, at the high end of the grades 2–3 text complexity band independently and proficiently.	By the end of year, read and comprehend informational texts, including history/social studies, science, and technical texts, in the grades 4–5 text complexity band proficiently, with scaffolding as needed at the high end of the range.	By the end of the year, read and comprehend informational texts, including history/social studies, science, and technical texts, at the high end of the grades 4–5 text complexity band independently and proficiently.

Grade 6	Grade 7	Grade 8
By the end of the year, read and comprehend literary nonfiction in the grades 6–8 text complexity band proficiently, with scaffolding as needed at the high end of the range.	By the end of the year, read and comprehend literary nonfiction in the grades 6–8 text complexity band proficiently, with scaffolding as needed at the high end of the range.	By the end of the year, read and comprehend literary nonfiction at the high end of the grades 6–8 text complexity band independently and proficiently.

Grades 9–10	Grades 11–12
By the end of grade 9, read and comprehend literary nonfiction in the grades 9–10 text complexity band proficiently, with scaffolding as needed at the high end of the range. By the end of grade 10, read and comprehend literary nonfiction at the high end of the grades 9–10 text complexity band independently and proficiently.	By the end of grade 11, read and comprehend literary nonfiction in the grades 11-CCR text complexity band proficiently, with scaffolding as needed at the high end of the range. By the end of grade 12, read and comprehend literary nonfiction at the high end of the grades 11-CCR text complexity band independently and proficiently.

Source: *http://www.corestandards.org/assets/CCSSI_ELA%20Standards.pdf*

COLLEGE AND CAREER READINESS STANDARDS IN A NUTSHELL

	STANDARD	BIG IDEA
Key Ideas and Details	CCR Standard 1	*Reading for Details Using Both Literal and Inferential Understanding*
	CCR Standard 2	*Theme and Main Idea and Summarization*
	CCR Standard 3	*Narrative Elements (Character, Setting, Plot) and Sequence of Events*
Craft and Structure	CCR Standard 4	*Vocabulary in Context*
	CCR Standard 5	*Text Structure*
	CCR Standard 6	*Point of View and Author's Purpose*
Integration of Knowledge and Ideas	CCR Standard 7	*Diverse Text Formats and Media*
	CCR Standard 8	*Evaluate Arguments in Nonfiction Text (Not applicable to literature)*
	CCR Standard 9	*Comparing and Contrasting Multiple Texts*
Range of Reading and Level of Text Complexity	CCR Standard 10	*A Variety of Genres and Text Complexity*

Appendix B

KUDOs: An Overview

What Are KUDOs?

K   What do students need to **know**?

U   What do students need to **understand**?

DO   What do students need to **do**?

Breaking Down KUDOs: An Introduction

Use the KUDOs framework as a continuum of student learning. As an essential component of differentiated instruction, KUDOs provide a powerful method for educators to deconstruct the anchor standards into distinct, manageable, progressive chunks. KUDOs' progressive acquisition of learning is highlighted by its alignment to Bloom's Taxonomy (1956), which illustrates how learning gradually gains in cognitive rigor and application. Taken as a whole, KUDOs aid in planning for RtI and delivering prescriptive, scaffolded teaching to meet the unique needs of all students.

Using KUDOs as a framework, educators first consider what factual knowledge students must KNOW in order to build their abilities within that anchor standard. This first piece of the framework is critical because if students lack the basic vocabulary and facts of the standard, their ability to learn and acquire the necessary skill set for that standard will be significantly impaired. For example, a student who does not know what the term *theme* means cannot possibly understand its purpose in literature.

If students possess this basic knowledge, instruction should move toward what students must UNDERSTAND, or the big ideas and concepts inherent within the

Targeted Reading Interventions for the Common Core © 2014 by Diana Sisson & Betsy Sisson, Scholastic Teaching Resources

anchor standard. At this stage of learning acquisition, students already possess the core knowledge of the skill, but they struggle with what to do with this knowledge and why it is important to them as readers. Returning to the previous example, students may be able to recite the definition of *theme*, but if they are unable to grasp that narrative elements contribute to the development of the theme, then they will, in turn, fail to develop the skill set necessary to identify themes independently.

After ensuring that students both know and understand key aspects of the anchor standard, educators, only then, should transition toward what students are expected to DO. In the case of theme, possessing a clear definition of theme and equipped with underlying "big ideas" about theme, they are now prepared and confident enough to determine the theme of a given text.

This framework, then, not only allows educators to deconstruct the anchor standards into progressive learning stages, but it also reinforces the understanding that students who struggle cannot be rushed into independently performing applications of anchor standards (e.g., identifying a theme in a given text) without first carefully starting at the foundational level and developing their skill set. Too often, we rush to expect students to demonstrate their knowledge without first providing careful, scaffolded instruction that gradually builds their skills at a pace that is conducive to their learning needs. The KUDOs framework addresses this concern and ensures that students who struggle receive the scaffolding they need to become independent readers and thinkers.

KNOW	UNDERSTAND	DO
Vocabulary	Concepts	Skills
Facts	Generalizations	Applications
What students need to memorize for the standard	What "big idea" students need to take away from the standard	What students need to be able to do independently with the standard
Bloom's Taxonomy: Knowledge	*Bloom's Taxonomy:* Understand	*Bloom's Taxonomy:* Application Analysis Synthesis Evaluation

Appendix C: Additional Resources

Information at a Glance

Common Core State Standards & Assessment

- Common Core State Standards Web site: **http://www.corestandards.org** (Provides the standards, frequently asked questions, and parent resources)

- Council of Chief State School Officers (CCSSO) Web site: **http://www.ccsso.org/ Resources/Digital_Resources/Common_Core_Implementation_Video_Series. html** (Presents a series of video vignettes to explain the standards in greater depth)

- Smarter Balanced Assessment Consortium Web site: **http://www. smarterbalanced.org** (Contains descriptions of the assessments, practice tests, and released items as well as Common Core State Standards tools and resources for member states belonging to the Smarter Balanced Assessment Consortium)

- Partnership for Assessment of Readiness for College and Careers (PARCC) Assessment Consortium Web site: **http://www.parcconline.org** (Contains descriptions of the assessments, practice tests, sample questions, resources, and updates for member states belonging to the PARCC Assessment Consortium)

Special Interest Groups

- International Reading Association (IRA) Web site: **http://www.reading.org** (Offers books, journals, and resources focused on literacy instruction)

- Teachers of English to Speakers of Other Languages (TESOL) International Organization Web site: **http://www.tesol.org** (Supplies articles, books, tools, and resources for second-language learners)

- National Center for Learning Disabilities (NCLD) Web site: **http://www.ncld. org** (Aligns instructional resources and parent support for students with learning disabilities)

- Council for Exceptional Children (CEC) Web site: **http://www.cec.sped.org** (Recommends best practices for supporting special education students)

Parent Resources

- National Parent Teacher Association (PTA) Web site: **http://www.pta.org/ parents/content.cfm?ItemNumber=2910** (Furnishes brief parent guides by individual grades that explain the Common Core State Standards, delineate what is expected academically at that grade level, highlight what parents can do at home to support their children, and recommend techniques to build a strong home-school relationship; guides are available in both English and Spanish)

- Council of the Great City Schools (CGCS) Web site: **http://www.cgcs.org/ Page/328** (Furnishes expanded parent guides by grade level that explain what is expected of students academically with the Common Core State Standards—with both literature and informational text—and places the grade levels in context by illustrating expectations from the previous grade as well as the upcoming grade; also suggests ways parents can help their children learn outside of school; guides are available in both English and Spanish)

Instruction Resources

- Achieve the Core Web site: **http://www.achievethecore.org** (Offers a range of supports, including lesson plans, student writing samples, assessment questions, curricular tools, techniques for supporting all students, and professional development)

- Association for Supervision and Curriculum Development (ASCD) Web site: **http:// educore.ascd.org** (Makes available a collection of tools, strategies, videos, and resources specifically designed for implementing Common Core State Standards)

Student Reading Materials

(*Literature, Informational Text, Drama, and Poetry*)

- Clarkness.com: **http://www.clarkness.com/index.htm** (Delivers hundred of free stories and e-books for the beginning reader)

- Dr. Young's Reading Room (Texas A & M University): **http://www.thebestclass. org/rtscripts.html** (Furnishes Readers Theater scripts)

- Giggle Poetry: **http://www.gigglepoetry.com/** (Provides a range of fun poems for the primary student)

- Harvard Classics: **http://www.bartleby.com/17/1/** (Makes available over 80 of Aesop's fables)

- Internet4Classrooms: **http://www.internet4classrooms.com/grade_level_ help.htm** (Grants access to grade-level skill builders and Common Core-aligned stories, activities, and resources)

- NEWSELA: **http://www.newsela.com** (Presents current events texts at a range of grade levels and lexiles—educators can select a text and then raise or lower the grade level/lexile based on the needs of their students; also aligned to Common Core State Standards.)

- Read Me a Story, Ink: **http://www.readmeastoryink.com/index.php** (Supplies over 1,000 read-aloud short stories and book recommendations with a search feature by story category and grade)

Glossary of Terms

Below is a glossary of key vocabulary terms related to the anchor standards. Definitions have been simplified for classroom instructional use.

Alliteration: Repetition of initial consonant sounds; example: *Peter Piper picked a peck of peppers.*

Allusion: A reference to a person, place, or event (real or fictionalized)

Analogy: A comparison of two things upon which comparisons may be made

Author: The person who wrote the text

Central message: Synonymous with theme or lesson; see "Theme"

Character: The person or animal in a story; characters can be described through both direct (what the author actually says) and indirect characterization (what the characters do, say, think, feel or look like).

Connotative meanings: Words associated with a term; example: *The terms* gentleman, dude, *and* guy *are connotative words associated with* man.

Dialogue: Conversation between two or more characters

Digital text: Electronic version of a printed text

Drama: A serious narrative; a play

Drawing conclusions: The synthesis of facts and the reader's prior knowledge to infer relationships, judge occurrences, and predict events

Explicit: Clearly stated

Event: A specific thing that happens in the story; individual events help propel the story forward; this can best be explained by answering the following questions: What happened first? Then what happened? What happened next? How did the story end?

Evidence: Details that prove conclusion or judgment

Fable: A fictionalized story that contains animals as characters and attempts to teach a moral, or lesson, to the reader; example: *"The Lion and the Mouse" from Aesop's fables*

Fantasy story: A fictionalized story that contains magic or supernatural characteristics; example: *the Harry Potter series by J. K. Rowling*

Fiction: A made-up text created by an author

Figurative language: A description of something made through comparisons; typically requires the reader to use his or her imagination; examples: *simile, metaphor, onomatopoeia, personification, alliteration, hyperbole*

Flashback: A part of a narrative that occurs when the author suddenly interrupts the flow of the story to jump back to earlier events; example: *a story begins when a person is quite old, but then jumps backward in time to when he or she was a child.*

Folktale: A fictionalized story that has been orally passed down through generations of a people

Historical novel: A fictionalized story set in an actual period of history; example: The Midwife's Apprentice *by Karen Cushman (1995)*

Hyperbole: An exaggeration so great as not to be believed; example: *The students have a mountain of homework.*

Illustration: A picture in a text

Illustrator: A person who creates pictures for a text

Inference: A conclusion based on reasoning from evidence

Irony: The contrast between what is expected and what actually exists or happens; example: *It would be ironic if a champion swimmer hated to swim.*

Lesson: Synonymous with central message or theme; see "Theme"

Media: Means of communication; examples: *printed text, electronic text, audio recording, videotaped production*

Metaphor: A comparison of unlike things without using the words *like* or *as*; example: *She is a rose.*

Meter: The measured arrangement of words in poetry

Moral: Synonymous with theme or lesson; see "Theme"

Multimedia: The combined use of several media forms

Mythology: Fictionalized stories from ancient times that attempt to explain the natural world; example: *the Greek myth of Demeter and the changing seasons*

Narrator: The person who tells the story

Targeted Reading Interventions for the Common Core © 2014 by Diana Sisson & Betsy Sisson, Scholastic Teaching Resources

Opinion: A belief about something

Onomatopoeia: A word that describes or imitates a sound from nature; example: *A snake hisses.*

Personification: An animal or object that takes on human characteristics; example: *The wind whistled in the trees.*

Poem: A text meant to convey ideas and emotions, typically using rhyme, rhythm, and meter

Poetry: A text containing qualities found in poems

Point of view: How an author decides to tell a story; example: *Who is telling the story? If you see the words "I," "me," or "we," then it's a first-person point of view; if you see the words "you" or "your," then it's a second-person point of view; if you see the words "he," "she," or "they," then it's a third-person point of view.*

Plot: The main events of a story; a well-developed plot has a cause-and-effect pattern—one event naturally leads to another

Problem: An obstacle that prevents a character from reaching his or her goal; stories must have problems—without the characters experiencing a problem, the story lacks interest.

Prose: A piece of text that uses everyday written language—in contrast to poetry, which utilizes a metrical structure; prose encompasses literature, informational text, and drama.

Purpose: The reason an author writes something

Resolution: A solution to the problem in a story

Rhyme: A regular matching of sounds, typically at the end of words; example: *dog and frog*

Rhythm: A pattern of recurring sounds

Sarcasm: The use of words to mean the opposite of what is actually said

Satire: A fictionalized text that attempts to highlight human weakness or vice and ridicule it

Scene: The division in a play that encompasses a single unit of development within the plot of the story

Section: A major part of a text

Setting: The time and place in which story events happen; the setting can be determined through looking at the styles of buildings, transportation, language, and clothing described in the text.

Simile: A comparison of unlike things using the words *like* or *as*; example: *She is as pretty as a rose.*

Soliloquy: A dramatic discourse in which a character talks to himself or herself and reveals his or her thoughts

Solution: How the problem in the plot is resolved; the problem in the story must be resolved in some way—the reader may not like the solution, but a solution of some nature must exist.

Sonnet: A poem comprised of 14 lines and typically expressing one central theme or idea

Stanza: A division of a poem with at least two lines, usually characterized by a common meter and rhyme

Summarize: To group main points together to form a short, clear understanding of a text; to summarize effectively, distinguish between ideas that the author deems important and those that are interesting but secondary; also differentiate between main ideas (something repeated throughout the text) and details (something found only once or twice in the text).

Supporting details: The individual parts of the whole text that contribute to the main idea or central idea

Technical meanings: Specialized vocabulary in a given field

Text: Written or printed words

Text structure: How information is organized; (1) main idea text structure presents important information on a specific topic and gives characteristics about that topic; (2) sequence of events text structure presents a number of ideas or events in a succession; (3) compare/contrast text structure presents likenesses and differences between two objects or ideas; (4) cause/effect text structure presents ideas so that reasons and consequences can be identified.

Textual evidence: Details from a text that support the conclusion drawn by the reader

Theme: A lesson a story teaches

Tone: The atmosphere that the writer creates in his story; example: *Ask yourself how the story makes you feel? Joyful? Sad? Hopeful?*

Topic: The subject of a text

Traditional literature: Literature that has existed in a culture for a long period of time; see "Folktale"

Verse: A single line of poetry

References

Afflerbach, P., & Cho, B. (2009). Identifying and describing constructively responsive comprehension strategies in new and traditional forms of reading. In S. E. Israel & G. G. Duffy (Eds.). *Handbook of research on reading comprehension*. New York: Routledge.

Alvermann, D. E., Swafford, J., & Montero, M. K. (2004). *Content area literacy instruction for the elementary grades*. Boston: Allyn & Bacon.

Armbruster, B., Lehr, F., Osborne, J., & Adler, C. R. (2010). *Put reading first: The research building blocks for teaching children to read: Kindergarten through grade three*. Washington, D.C.: National Institute for Literacy.

Artley, A. S. (1943). Teaching word-meaning through context. *The Elementary English Review, 20*(2), 68–74.

Ash, G. E. (2005). What did Abigail mean? *Educational Leadership, 63*(2), 36-41.

Bakken, J. P., & Whedon, C. K. (2002). Teaching text structure to improve reading comprehension. *Intervention in school and clinic, 37*(4), 229–233. doi: 10.1177/105345120203700406

Barnes, A. C., & Harlacher, J. E. (2008). Clearing the confusion: Response-to-intervention as a set of principles. *Education and Treatment of Children, 31*(3), 417–431.

Basaraba, D., Yovanoff, P., Alonzo, J., & Tindal, G. (2013). Examining the structure of reading comprehension: Do literal, inferential, and evaluative comprehension truly exist? *Reading & Writing, 26*, 349–379. doi:10.1007/s11145-012-9372-9

Baumann, J. F. (2005). Vocabulary-comprehension relationships. In B. Maloch, J. V. Hoffman, D. L. Schallert, C. M. Fairbanks, & J. Worthy (Eds.). *Fifty-fourth yearbook of the National Reading Conference* (pp. 117–131). Oak Creek, WI: National Reading Conference.

Baumann, J. F., Kame'enui, E.J., & Ash, G.E. (2003). Research on vocabulary instruction: Voltaire redux. In J. Flood, D. Lapp, J.R. Squire, & J.M. Jensen (Eds.). *Handbook of research on teaching the English language arts* (2nd ed.). (pp. 752–785). Mahwah, NJ: Lawrence Erlbaum Associates.

Beck, I. L., & McKeown, M. G. (2007). Increasing young low-income children's oral vocabulary repertoires through rich and focused instruction. *Elementary School Journal, 107*, 251–273.

Bloom, B. S. (Ed.). (1956). *Taxonomy of educational objectives: Book 1 cognitive domain*. White Plains, NY: Longman.

Brabham, E. G., & Villaume, S. K. (2002). Leveled text: The good news and the bad news. *The Reading Teacher, 55*(5), 438–441.

Bråten, I., Britt, M. A., Strømsø, H. I., & Rouet, J. (2011). The role of epistemic beliefs in the comprehension of multiple expository texts: Toward an integrated model. *Educational Psychologies, 46*(1), 48–70. doi: 10.1080/00461520.2011.538647

Bukowiecki, E. M., & McMackin, M. C. (1999). Young children and narrative texts: A school-based inquiry project. *Reading Improvement, 36*(4), 157–166.

Bus, A. G., & Neuman, S. B. (2009). *Multimedia and literacy development: Improving achievement for young learners*. New York: Taylor & Francis.

Calkins, L. M. (1994). *The art of teaching writing*. Portsmouth, NH: Heinemann, 1994.

Carlisle, J. F. (2007). Fostering morphological processing, vocabulary development, and reading comprehension. In R. K. Wagner, A. E. Muse, & K. R. Tannenbaum (Eds.). *Vocabulary acquisition: Implications for reading comprehension*. New York: The Guilford Press.

Ciampa, K. (2012). I CAN READ: The effects of an online reading program on grade 1 students' engagement and comprehension strategy use. *Journal of Research on Technology in Education, 45*(1), 27–59.

Coiro, J. (2003). Reading comprehension on the internet: Expanding our understanding of reading comprehension to encompass new literacies. *The Reading Teacher, 56*(5), 458–464.

Coiro, J., Knobel, M., Lankshear, C., & Leu, D. J. (Ed.). (2008). *Handbook of research on new literacies*. New York: Taylor & Francis.

Colby, S. A., & Lyon, A. F. (2004). Heightening awareness about the importance of using multicultural literature. *Multicultural Education, 11*(3), 24–28.

Coleman, D. (2011). *David Coleman: Common Core: Summer 2011*. [Audio podcast]. Retrieved from http://www.youtube.com/watch?v=aTCiQVCpdQc

Cushman, K. (1995). *The midwife's apprentice*. New York: Clarion Books.

Davis, F. B. (1944). Fundamental factors of comprehension of reading. *Psychometrika, 9*, 185–197.

Duke, N. K. (2007). Let's look in a book: Using nonfiction texts for reference with young children. *Young Children, 62*(3), 12–16.

Duke, N. K., Bennett-Armistead, V. S., & Roberts, E. M. (2002). Incorporating informational text in primary grades. In C. M. Roller (Ed.). *A collection of papers from the reading research 2001 conference* (pp. 40–54). Newark, DE: International Reading Association.

Duke, N. K., Caughlan, S., Juzwik, M. M., & Martin, N. M. (2012). Teaching genre with purpose. *Educational Leadership, 69*(6), 34–39.

Duke, N. K., & Pearson, P. D. (2002). Effective practices for developing reading comprehension. In A. E. Farstrup & S. J. Samuels (Eds.). *What research has to say about reading instruction* (pp. 205–242). Newark, DE: International Reading Association.

Duke, N. K., & Roberts, K. M. (2010). The genre-specific nature of reading comprehension. In D. Wyse, R. Andrews, & J. Hoffman (Eds.). *The Routledge international handbook of English, language and literacy teaching* (pp. 74–86). London: Routledge.

Dymock, S. (2007). Comprehension strategy instruction: Teaching narrative text structure awareness. *The Reading Teacher, 61*(2), 161–167. doi: 10.1598/RT.61.2.6

Ebe, A. E. (2010). Culturally relevant texts and reading assessment for English language learners. *Reading Horizons, 50*(3), 193–210.

Fisher, D., & Frey, N. (2012). Close reading in elementary schools. *The Reading Teacher, 66*(3), 179–188. doi: 10.1002/TRTR.01117

Fisher, D., Frey, N., & Lapp, D. (2012). *Text complexity: Raising rigor in reading*. Newark, DE: International Reading Association.

Freebody, P., & Luke, A. (1990). "Literacies" programs: Debates and demands in cultural context. *Prospect, 5*(5) 7–16.

Fuchs, D., Fuchs, L. S., & Vaughn, S. (Eds.). (2008). *Response to Intervention: A framework for reading educators*. Newark, DE: International Reading Association.

Fukkink, R. J., & de Glopper, J., (1998). Effects of instruction in deriving word meaning from context: A meta-analysis. *Review of Educational Research, 68*(4), 450–469. doi: 10.3102/00346543068004450

Fulton, L., & Poeltler, E. (2013). Developing a scientific argument. *Science & Children, 59*(9), 30–35.

Gewertz, C. (2013). Global study identifies promising practices in top-scoring nations. *Education Week, 33*(7), p. 9.

Gill, S. R. (2008). The comprehension matrix: A tool for designing comprehension instruction. *The Reading Teacher, 62*(2), 106–113. doi: DOI: 10.1598/RT.62.2.2

Goetz, S., & Walker, B. J. (2004). At-risk readers can construct complex meanings: Technology can help. *The Reading Teacher, 57*(8), 778–780.

Gomez-Zwiep, S., & Harris, D. (2010). Supporting ideas with evidence. *Science & Children, 48*(1), 76–79.

Goodman, K. S. (1965). A linguistic study of cues and miscues in reading. *Elementary English, 42,* 639–643.

Graves, M. F., & Watts-Taffe, S. M. (2002). The place of word consciousness in a research-based vocabulary program. In A. E. Farstrup & S. J. Samuels, (Eds.). *What research has to say about reading instruction.* Newark, DE: International Reading Association.

Greenwood, C. R., Kamps, D., Terry, B. J., & Linebarger, D. L. (2007). Primary intervention: A means of preventing special education? In D. Haager, J. Klinger, & S. Vaughn (Eds.). *Evidence-based reading practices for Response to Intervention* (pp. 73–106). Baltimore: Paul H. Brookes Publishing Co.

Griffith, P. L., & Ruan, J. (2005). What is metacognition and what should be its role in literacy instruction? In S. E. Israel, C. C. Block, K. L. Bauserman, & Kinnucan-Welsch, K. (Eds.). *Metacognition in literacy learning: Theory, assessment, instruction, and professional development.* Mahwah: NJ: Lawrence Erlbaum.

Hall, K., Sabey, B., & McClellan, M. (2005). Expository text structure: Helping primary-grade teachers use expository texts to full advantage. *Reading Psychology: An International Quarterly, 26*(3), 211–234.

Harvey, S., & Goudvis, A. (2000). *Strategies that work: Teaching comprehension for understanding and engagement.* Portland, ME: Stenhouse.

Heacox, D. (2009). *Making differentiation a habit.* Minneapolis, MN: Free Spirit Publishing, Inc.

Heisey, N., & Kucan, L. (2010). Introducing science concepts to primary students through read-alouds: Interactions and multiple texts make the difference. *The Reading Teacher, 6*(8), 666–676.

Herber, H. L. (1970). *Teaching reading in the content areas.* Englewood Cliffs, NJ: Prentice Hall.

Hiebert, E. H., & Pearson, P. D. (2010). *An examination of current text difficulty indices with early reading texts.* (Reading Research Report #10-01). San Francisco: TextProject, Inc.

Johnson, J. C. (2005). What makes a "good" reader? Asking students to define "good" readers. *The Reading Teacher, 58*(8), 766–770. doi: 10.1598/RT.58.8.6

Juel, C., & Deffes, R. (2004). Making words stick. *Educational Leadership, 61*(6), 30–34.

Keene, E. O., & Zimmermann, S. (1997). *Mosaic of thought.* Portsmouth, NH: Heinemann.

Kieffer, M. J., & Lesaux, N. K. (2007). Breaking down words to build meanings: Morphology, vocabulary and reading comprehension in the urban classroom. *The Reading Teacher, 61*(2), 134–144. doi: 10.1598/RT.61.2.3

Kintsch, W., & Rawson, K. A. (2005). Comprehension. In M. J. Snowling & C. Hulme (Eds.). *The science of reading: A handbook* (pp. 209–226). Malden, MA: Blackwell.

Kruse, M. (2001). Escaping ethnic encapsulation: The role of multicultural children's literature. *Delta Kappa Gamma Bulletin, 67*(2), 26–32.

Kuzminski, P. (2002). The effective use of literature in preparing children for a global society. *Delta Kappa Gamma Bulletin, 69*(1), 19–22.

Leu, Jr., D. J. (2000). Our children's future: Changing the focus of literacy and literacy instruction. *The Reading Teacher, 53*(5), 424–429.

Louie, B. Y. (2011). Guiding principles for teaching multicultural literature. *The Reading Teacher, 59*(5), 438–448. doi: 10.1598RT.59.5.3

Lubliner, S., & Smetana, L. (2005). The effects of comprehensive vocabulary instruction on Title I students' metacognitive word-learning skills and reading comprehension. *Journal of Literacy Research, 37,* 163–200.

Lyon, G. R. (1998). Overview of reading and literacy research. In S. Patton & M. Holmes (Eds.). *The keys to literacy.* Washington, D.C.: Council for Basic Education.

McGregor, T. (2007). *Comprehension connections: Bridges to strategic reading.* Portsmouth, NH: Heinemann.

Mahdavi, J., & Tensfeldt, L. (2013). Untangling reading comprehension strategy instruction: Assisting struggling readers in the primary grades. *Preventing School Failure, 57*(2), 77–92.

Mellard, D. E., & Johnson, E. (2008). *RtI: A practitioner's guide to implementing Response to Intervention.* Thousand Oaks, CA: Corwin Press.

Mesmer, H. A., Cunningham, J. W., & Hiebert, E. H. (2012). Toward a theoretical model of text complexity for the early grades: Learning from the past, anticipating the future. *Reading Research Quarterly, 47*(3), 235–258. doi: 10.1002/rrq.019

Meyer, B. J. F. (1987). Following the author's top-level organization: An important skill for reading comprehension. In R. J. Tierney, P. L. Anders, & J. N. Mitchell (Eds.). *Understanding readers' understanding: Theory and practice,* (pp. 59–76). Hillsdale, NJ: Lawrence Erlbaum.

Meyer, B. J. F., & Ray, M. N. (2011). Structure strategy interventions: Increasing reading comprehension of expository text. *International Electronic Journal of Elementary Education, 4*(1), 127–152.

Miller, D. (2002). *Reading with meaning: Teaching comprehension in the primary grades.* Portland, ME: Stenhouse.

Molden, K. (2007). Critical literacy, the right answer for the reading classroom: Strategies to move beyond comprehension for reading comprehension. *Reading Improvement, 44*(1), 50–56.

Moss, B. (2011). Making a case and a place for effective content area literacy instruction in the elementary grades. *The Reading Teacher, 59*(1), 46–55. doi: 10.1598

Nagy, W. E., & Anderson, R. C. (1987). Learning word meanings from context during normal reading. *American Educational Research Journal, 24*(2), 237–270. doi: 10.3102/ 00028312024002237

Nation, K. (2005). Children's reading comprehension difficulties. In M. J. Snowling & C. Hulme (Eds.). *The science of reading: A handbook* (pp. 248–265). Malden, MA: Blackwell.

National Governors Association Center for Best Practices & Council of Chief State School Officers. (2010). Common Core State Standards for English language arts and literacy in history/social studies, science, and technical subjects. Washington, DC: Authors.

National Institute of Child Health and Student Development, *Report of the National Reading Panel. Teaching children to read: An evidence-based assessment of scientific research literature on reading and its implications for reading instruction.* (2000). *(NIH Publication No. 00-4769).* Washington, DC: U.S. Government Printing Office.

Neuman, S. B., & Roskos, K. (2012). How children become more knowledgeable through text. *The Reading Teacher, 66*(3), 207–210. doi: 10.1002/TRTR.01118

Nussbaum, E. M. (2008). Collaborative discourse, argumentation, and learning: Preface and literature review. *Contemporary Educational Psychology, 33*(3), 345–359.

Ogle, D., & Blachowicz, C. L. Z. (2002). Beyond literature circles: Helping students comprehend information texts. In C. C. Block & M. Pressley (Eds.). *Comprehension instruction: Research-based best practices.* New York: The Guilford Press.

Pantaleo, S. (2005). "Reading" young children's visual texts. *Early Childhood Research & Practice, 7*(1). [Electronic version].

Pardo, L. S. (2004). What every teacher needs to know about comprehension. *The Reading Teacher, 58*(3), 272–280. doi: 10.1598/RT.58.3.5

Paul, R., & Elder, L. (2003). Critical thinking. . . and the art of close reading (Part 1). *Journal of Developmental Education, 27*(2), 36–37, 39.

Perfetti, C. A., Marron, M. A., & Foltz, P. W. (1996). Sources of comprehension failure: Theoretical perspectives and case studies. In C. Cornoldi & J. Oakhill (Eds.). *Reading comprehension difficulties: Processes and intervention* (pp. 137–165). Mahwah, NJ: Lawrence Erlbaum.

Ranker, J. (2011). Learning nonfiction in an ESL class: The interaction of situated practice and teacher scaffolding in a genre study. *The Reading Teacher, 62*(7), 580–589. doi: 10.1598/RT.62.7.4

Reese, E., Suggate, D., Long, J., & Schaughency, E., (2010). Children's oral narrative and reading skills in the first 3 years of reading instruction. *Reading and Writing, 23*, 627–644. doi: 10.1007/s11145-009-9175-9

Richek, M. (2005). Words are wonderful: Interactive, time-efficient strategies to teach meaning vocabulary. *The Reading Teacher, 58*(5), 414–423.

Rouet, J., Lowe, R., Schnotz, W. (Eds.). (2008). *Understanding multimedia documents.* New York: Springer.

Scarborough, H. (2001). Connecting early language and literacy to later reading (dis) abilities: Evidence, theory, and practice. In S. B. Neuman & D. Dickinson (Eds.). *Handbook of early literacy research* (pp. 97–110). New York: The Guilford Press.

Shanahan, T., Fisher, D., & Frey, N. (2012). The challenge of challenging text. *Educational Leadership, 69*(6), 58–63.

Sisson, D., & Sisson, B. (2014). *Close reading in elementary school: Bringing readers and texts together.* New York: Taylor & Francis.

Smith, C. B. (1994). *Helping children understand literary genres.* Bloomington, IN: ERIC Clearinghouse on Reading, English, and Communication. (Document # ED366985).

Smith, N. B. (1974). The classroom teacher's responsibility to the disabled reader. Paper presented at the International Reading Association World Congress on Reading, Vienna, Austria. Abstract retrieved from http://files.eric.ed.gov/fulltext/ED095496.pdf

Snow, C. E. (2002). *Reading for understanding: Toward a R&D program in reading comprehension.* Santa Monica, CA: RAND.

Stahl, S., & Nagy, W. (2006). *Teaching word meanings.* Mahwah, NJ: Lawrence Erlbaum.

Sternberg, R. J. (1987). Most vocabulary is learned from context. In M. G. McKeown & M. E. Curtis (Eds.). *The nature of vocabulary acquisition,* (pp. 89–105). Hillsdale, NJ: Lawrence Erlbaum.

Stetter, M. E., & Hughes, M. T. (2010). Using story grammar to assist students with learning disabilities and reading difficulties improve their comprehension. *Education and Treatment of Children, 33*(1), 115–151. doi: 10.1353/etc.0.0087

Stobaugh, R. (2013). *How to teach students to evaluate information: A key common core skill.* Larchmont, NY: Eye on Education.

Taylor, L. K., Abler, S. R., & Walker D. W. (2002). The comparative effects of a modified self-questioning strategy and story mapping on the reading comprehension of elementary students with learning disabilities. *Journal of Behavioral Education, 11*(2), 69–87.

Taylor, S. V. (2000). Multicultural is who we are: Literature as a reflection of ourselves. *Teaching Exceptional Children, 32*(3), 24–29.

Van Kleeck, A. (2008). Providing preschool foundations for later reading comprehension: The importance of and ideas for targeting inferencing in storybook-sharing interventions. *Psychology in the Schools, 45*(7), 627–643. doi: 10.1002/pits.20314

Voss, J. F., & Wiley, J. (2000). A case study of developing historical understanding via instruction. In P. N. Stearns, P. Seixas, & S. Wineburg (Eds.). *Knowing, Teaching, and learning history: National and international perspectives* (pp. 375–389). New York: York University Press.

Vygotsky, L. S. (1962). *Thought and language.* (E. Hanfmann & G. Vakar, Eds. & Trans.). Cambridge, MA: MIT.

Vygotsky, L. S. (1978). *Mind in society: The development of higher psychological processes.* Cambridge, MA: Harvard University Press.

White, C. E. & Kim, J. S. (2009). *Putting the pieces of the puzzle together: How systematic vocabulary instruction and expanded learning time can address the literacy gap.* Washington, D.C.: Center for American Progress.

Williams, J. P. (2005). Instruction in reading comprehension for primary-grade students: A focus on text structure. *The Journal of Special Education, 39*(1), 6–18.

Williams, J., Hall, K., & Lauer, K. (2004). Teaching expository text structure to young at-risk learners: Building the basics of comprehension instruction. *Exceptionality, 12*(3), 129–144.